THE BRIDGE

PRAISE FOR
THE BRIDGE

"In his new work, *The Bridge*, Xavier guides us through the critical and necessary processes to cross the bridge toward our dreams, our goals and our deepest longings. The bridge cannot be crossed without a war, and these pages give us the strategy to win that war. May you have the courage to cross the bridge so that you can have the virtue of living a great life."

—ERWIN RAPHAEL MCMANUS
Founder of Mosaic and bestselling author of
The Last Arrow and *The Way of the Warrior*.
Los Angeles, California

"Practically every failure in life is the result of a lack of preparation. But my friend, Xavier, has written the blueprints in *The Bridge* to carry you from wishing to achieving! This book is an answer to prayer!"

—BISHOP DALE C. BRONNER
Founder/Senior Pastor, Word of Faith Family Worship Cathedral

"Each day there is a battle to be won. Each day we are fighting against something, whether it's a fight within us or outside of us. Xavier Cornejo is a leadership and life strategist. In *The Bridge*, he teaches us how to develop strategies, whom to listen to for such strategies and how to carry out the strategies that will help us conquer the wars of life, whether they be emotional, financial, relational or professional in nature. Thank you, Xavier, for this book; it is so important for the times in which we live."

—TIAGO BRUNET
International Motivational Speaker, Author of bestsellers, Brazil

"Life itself is a bridge. We start on one side and end up on the other, but not always the one we desired. The reason being, that if we go through life without a strategy, then we will make the wrong connections and cross life's bridges strenuously. *The Bridge* will help you choose wisely the army to surround yourself with in each battle you will face to lead to your dreams. Battles are not meant to be our end; they are meant to awaken the warrior that lies within us. Thank you, Xavier, for the valuable tools embodied in this book."

—KARLA PINEDA
TV Personality

"Sensational! *The Bridge* is a book that invites you to dream of new horizons, while also teaching you to daily create an atmosphere of strategies to help you fulfill your dreams. I am fully convinced that this book will give you the tools you need to reach the summit and live in it."

—EMERSON NOWOTNY
Pastor of Mosaic Church México

"Xavier is one of those people who can help part the seas in your life, thanks to his incredible ability to see potential in others, what they can achieve or reach even when they don't believe in it themselves. It turns out that, while the world tried to adapt to a new rhythm of life in the middle of the pandemic, Xavier decided to gift us this treasure of a book—*The Bridge*—to remind us that the dreams we have been given are meant to be worked and pursued, no matter how our surroundings may look. Not only does he remind us of that, but he also kindly pens on these pages an invaluable guide to trace the journey that will help us reach our new destinies.

The Bridge is an indispensable book, now more than ever, to chase after our dreams! Thank you, Xavier."

—VIVIANA SERNA
Movie, Theater and TV Actress

"I know very few people whose words and ideas resonate in my mind for days; they penetrate my soul and awaken my creativity. Xavier is one of those people. His book, *The Bridge: From Possibility to Reality*, is only one example of that. It's a manual of inspiration that invites us to dream, takes our hand and leads us to find the path of strategies and the plan that will turn our dreams into realities.

We all dare to dream. Some have the courage to fight for their dreams, but few have the wisdom to conquer them. This book has beautiful, clear and eloquent concepts that will lead you to practical steps to reach your dreams, not by luck but through predetermined decisions."

—Luis Ernesto Franco
Actor and Producer

"Xavier is one of the brightest minds I know. During the dinner we shared, I simply sat there and listened to him, without uttering a word. I felt that was the wisest thing I could do.

My grandfather and father were philosophers, and I am a fervent admirer of brilliant minds. A few days after I spoke with him, my whole world came crumbling down. My record label began to fall apart, financially, professionally and emotionally, and with it went my entire being. The crisis and mental pressure I felt made me physically sick.

On the same day that I wrote these words, I got the news that one of my friends passed away. The exhaustion that I felt pushed me to fall into a deep sleep, disconnected from everything. I woke up at two a.m., a bit scared and sad, and my spirit nudged me to read what Xavier had sent to me.

I read it slowly, paying attention to each word, as they slowly penetrated my soul. I regained energy and thought, *My record label needs to read this.* I know that all who do will come out stronger than ever before.

Thank you, Xavier, for encouraging my soul. *The Bridge* is a blessing."

—Kalimba
Author, Singer-songwriter, Producer and Businessman

"Part of knowing how to leverage our talents is losing that which most of us have abundantly: fear—namely, the fear of losing. How many things do we miss out on because of our fear of losing?

It takes a sensible person to get to know one's own talents and weaknesses; one can go years without being aware of them. Xavier has discovered the wonderful gifts God has given him and writes (as he says) not because his mind has something to say but because his soul has something to share.

Congratulations for not having buried this talent because each book you write calls us to write a better story and have the courage to tell it."

—Daniela Vega
Founder, *Storybook* App

"Everyone needs a firm bridge to reach their goals in life. More than the desire to cross it, we must be prepared for the stumbling blocks we may encounter on our path.

The Bridge has already become one of my favorites as we come out of the stupor of and fears surrounding the pandemic. The words are delivered with great eloquence to help us wake up and understand that, beyond talent, we need strategy. The concepts penetrate our senses like a dagger and make us reconsider what we are doing with our time. It's easy to identify with the anecdotes that reassure us in a simple manner that nothing is impossible, no matter how big or crazy it may seem.

Speaking of pain and growth, *The Bridge* could not have come at a better time. Following a difficult year full of uncertainty that put us to the test, we are challenged to prepare to become the best version of ourselves. Thank you, Xavier, for helping me cross the bridge of mental wars that cloud our dreams."

—Joe Bonilla
CEO, Latinvasion

"I've always been taught about the importance of starting with the end in mind, to have precise goals and a clear vision of what I want to achieve personally and professionally. What results do I strive for? What is my goal? However, no one talks about the process of reaching that goal. What are the tools I need along the path? How do I handle the situations that will come my way that I cannot control?

In *The Bridge*, Xavier Cornejo traces the route so that this process that you start with courage may lead you to your goal with wisdom. He will give you the steps to fight each battle strategically, learning along the way.

It's a book that will take your hand and lead you to fulfill the purpose for which you were created, to live out the dreams to which you've always aspired, and inspire others to do the same.

Are you ready to cross the bridge? I will see you on the other side!"

—VERÓNICA AVILÉS
Author of *La magia de reinventarte*

"I uphold a full life, far away from individualism, anguish and anxiety—a serene life built on the knowledge of who I am and who I want to become. Thankfully, there are human beings like Xavier Cornejo, who, through his book, *The Bridge*, is giving his talents so that others can also pursue a life lived in confidence. This book lights the path for us to follow and, with certainty, reach our dreams. His wisdom will show you how to build your success beyond your talents and gifts. 'In this life, we are all students and teachers.'

Thank you, Xavier Cornejo, for being a great teacher committed to others' wellbeing."

—SILVIA CÁZARES
Founder and Partner of Sheló NABEL
Businesswoman, Teacher and Life Coach

"Xavier has been a special person in my life. His wisdom and advice have helped me so much in my career in the world of fashion. He is always challenging me to think beyond my talents and beyond how to endure in a place where wisdom and character are vital."

—CHRISTIAN FERRETTI
Senior Menswear Designer at Guess, Inc., Celebrity Stylist

Design by Felipe Paredes
Cover Designed by Becky Speer
Illustrations by Xavier Cuenca
Photography by Andrew van Tilborgh

Book originally published in Spanish under the title "El Puente: de la posiblidad a la realidad"
Translation services by God-First Arts Inc.

ISBN: 978-1-954089-12-9   1 2 3 4 5 6 7 8 9 10

Printed in the United States of America

XAVIER CORNEJO

THE BRIDGE

From Possibility to Reality

AVAIL

Dedication

Lucas, I have held your hand since your first breath, and I will do it until my last breath.

In life, there are many bridges to cross, places to go and moments to conquer. Nothing will make me happier than seeing you reach everything that you can imagine and your heart desires.

I know there will be battles to fight in order to make your dreams a reality. Be courageous, and never give up the fight for what you are longing to achieve. What I have learned along the way is what I share with you on these pages to help you walk in the direction of your destination.

Always have strategy as your ally so you can reach your every dream. But it should always be God Who guides your steps. You can be certain that I would hold you, help you and propel you with all of my heart and with all of my strength, and even if my strength fades away, you can find in these pages the encouragement that you may need so you can try and try again.

The way you look at me and the way you smile at me are forever engraved on my heart.

It doesn't matter what you do or which way you go; I will always be by your side.

Love you, Son.

Acknowledgments

Lucas, you may not know it yet, but you are my greatest inspiration to keep writing and keep walking. Your days, your ideas and your smiles are the lights that guide my life. Thank you for being patient with me. I am convinced that *The Bridge* would not exist if you were not in my life.

To my parents, Jimmy and Aída, who, through their exemplary courage, have taught me that if you can dream big, you can also cross The Bridge. Whenever they have reached the other side, they have extended their hands so that I too can cross the bridges toward my destiny. I will be forever grateful to you both; your daily encouragement is the strength that helps me each day.

Diego, Rossana, Ma Gracia, Victoria and Juan Manuel, thank you for always looking out for me. Your love has shortened the distance that separates us. Physically we may be far away, but our hearts are close together.

Carlos, Veronica, Carlitos, Amelia, Santiago José and Soafía, your lives bring joy to my life. Thank you for believing in me and for always being present; you are a gift from God.

Omar, Lian, and Stephanie, thank you for always taking good care of Lucas and for all the love you have for him. I couldn't do what I do if you didn't look after him the way you do. You have my deepest thanks.

Ofelia, I don´t know whether this book is yours or if it is mine. Thank you for your care for it and all the attention to details, both in the work space and in my every day. There are no doubts that I couldn't have written this book without you; you have thought about every single detail of it. Every person who reads *The Bridge* should know that you helped me cross The Bridge from my possibility to my reality. Thank you for your constant care. I deeply appreciate your help. You have a very important place in my heart and in my life.

Karla, I am sure that the light inside you illuminates the pages inside this book. Thank you for walking by my side and cheering me on as I was writing this book. Thank you for helping me to see more at all those times when I wanted to give up. The Bridge could not be crossed if you hadn't walked with me.

To whom I consider my mentors, Erwin McManus, Dale Bronner and Sam Chand, you have deposited more knowledge, wisdom and courage in my life that I am capable of assimilating. There are not enough words to give you thanks, not only for your willingness to teach me but for the deepness of your friendship. This book is a small sample of what you have sown in my life.

Mariana, your constant motivation is an important part of my days. Thank you for always being there, for your support, but above all, for never giving up and always going for more.

Claudio, thank you, my friend, for taking this project, for welcoming me to your home and for opening the doors of your heart. More than friends, you Jimena, Luca, Mateo and Ana Renata are family. We are going to keep crossing bridges together.

Martijn and Amy, thank you for trusting in me, in my words and for helping people cross The Bridge. Nobody would be able to read this book in English without your faith in me and in this book.

Becky, thank you for your constant feedback and your bright ideas, and thank you for the composition of such an amazing cover.

Cuki, thanks for the illustrations. Thank you for dreaming with me and for your disposition to work with me.

Caroline, I am grateful for your help with this manuscript, for understanding me and what I wanted to accomplish with this book. You certainly make me sound smarter in English than I really am.

To the whole AVAIL team, thank you for your constant efforts to make sure that *The Bridge* can be read, but beyond that, for making sure that The Bridge can be crossed.

To all the readers of this book, thank you for giving me the opportunity to be a part of your days.

Finally, thank you, God, for giving me the opportunity to breathe, to think and to create. Thank you for crossing the bridge to embrace humanity. There is nothing I could do if You weren't with me.

Contents

イエス

Foreword

Words. They all have meaning. They mean different things to different people in different contexts. For example, simple words like "house" or "car" conjure distinct mental pictures for everyone.

Strategy is such a word. It becomes nuanced, even mysterious. Strategy needs strategy. That's exactly the thrust of this book. My friend, Xavier Cornejo, removes the nuances, deconstructs the mystery and in a very straightforward manner lets us know he will personally guide you over *The Bridge*—from possibility to reality.

In my leadership journey, I have succumbed to a lack of strategy multiple times. Here are some of its manifestations and their solutions provided by Xavier:

- Unclear Destination: Once the destination is clear, the decisions are easy; you can't cross the bridge to your dreams without knowing clearly what you want.

- Lack of Mentors: You can't cross the bridge to your dreams alone; there are always people you will need. Some are ahead of you in life, and others will walk by your side, but both are necessary. People connect us to the future.

- Poor Planning: For Xavier, planning is focusing ideas on how to reach your goals. At first, all ideas are valid and could be on the table, and then you can refine them or join them together.

- Deficient Preparation: The end result of our lives is the result of our preparation. What are you preparing for?

- Unaccountability in Execution: As I wrote in my book, What's Shaking Your Ladder?, "Who's going to do what by when?"

- Ambiguous Evaluation: Evaluation helps us realize if the strategy we choose is taking us closer or farther from our goal.

- Weak Endurance: In order to cross the bridge, you need to endure the way. It's not always easy, and there will be pain.

- Impatience with Time: Crossing the bridge will take time. When developing a strategy, you need to calculate the time it could take. This will help remove some of the anxiety.

- Continuous Striving for Growth: There is no limit on the number of bridges you can cross, and there is no limit in what you will be able to do if you dedicate yourself to grow.

However, the good news is that in this book Xavier addresses all of the above, explains the wherewithal needed and gives you practical steps to your success. You'll wish you'd had this book earlier. I know I do. But let me assure you, it is just in time!

To your success …

SAM CHAND,
Leadership consultant and author of *Leadership Pain*

侍 NEVER GO TO WAR WITHOUT A STRATEGY.

XAVIER CORNEJO

Introduction

"Nothing happens until we have the courage to begin."

—XAVIER CORNEJO

"I don't even know how I lost," Adonis Creed said in disbelief.

"Your mind wasn't right. And your natural style won't work with a guy that big," Rocky answered.[1]

I have thought a lot about these words as they have echoed in my mind and soul.

It had only been a couple of weeks since I had finished writing my first book, *La Historia Dentro de ti—The Story Within You*—and I had promised myself I would never write again. The mental exhaustion of putting my soul on paper was real. However, as I listened to Rocky's words, an idea sparked like a flame within me. I have discovered that

---

1   From the movie *Creed II*, with Sylvester Stallone and Michael B. Jordan, MGM, 2018.

what burns inside of us is meant to illuminate the world around us. It is a spark that lights our path and reveals the bridge to our destiny. At that very moment, I understood that I do not write because my mind has something to say; I write because my soul has something to share.

Creed didn't just lose his first fight against Drago; he was knocked out. Technically, he officially won because his opponent was disqualified, but still—knocked out. Despite everything, Rocky's words are not ones of defeat. He does not say, "You will never succeed." He simply says, "Your natural style won't work with a guy that big."

In other words, to win the battle, it takes something more than just talent. That something is wisdom because wisdom prepares us for battle, and not all battles are created equal. Though there are battles that we can win with talent alone, the war is won with wisdom. Wisdom isn't preparing yourself so that life doesn't strike you down. Wisdom readies you to get back up when it does.

You need courage to begin but wisdom to finish. Talent can lead you to fights that can only be won with strategy.

I am convinced that the idea that sparked in my mind as I listened to Rocky's words was intertwined with something that I already had simmering in my heart before I even watched the movie. On September 9, 2018, I had read the story of an Israeli army commander whose name was Joshua. I know not whether I should admire him more for his constant courage or his remarkable wisdom.

There was a point in the story at which the Israelites had recently left the desert after wandering there for 40 years. Before that, they had been slaves in Egypt, and they were now in pursuit of the freedom they would find in the Promised Land.

As they embarked on their journey, they reached a city called Jericho. Jericho was surrounded by walls—a city that its enemies could not penetrate. Joshua's army was experienced in battle. However, it had never faced walls of this size. Joshua was a military man, so he did not merely attack the city and hope to conquer with talent alone when he arrived at the walls. He waited to develop a strategy.[2]

As I read this story and listened to Rocky's resonating words, "Your natural style won't work with a guy that big," the following words echoed in my mind and my heart:

Never go to war without a strategy.

Never before had seven words formed a phrase that burned so intensely within me.

Many of us try to fight battles using only our abilities, but one's *ability* can become a *debility* when *calculation* is not part of the *equation*. If your talent is enough to win the battle for your dreams, your dreams are too small. The greatest wars aren't won with talent alone. Wisdom is needed. Strategy is needed. A strategy is nothing more than thought-out steps that will lead you to your desired end.

There is a war being waged as we pursue our destinies—as we chase our dreams. With the passing of time and the sting of defeat lingering in our hearts, some of us have stopped pursuing our dreams. Now,

---

2   Joshua 6.

those dreams sit in a dusty and forgotten corner in our most treasured thoughts.

Many times, we think that harmony is the opposite of battle, and we abandon our dreams in an attempt to preserve it. If truth be told, harmony does not oppose battle because there is no harmony without a battle. Unless we fight the battle for our dreams, harmony will never be ours.

Some of us may be on the verge of surrender. Others keep fighting. The deepest problem with both is that we're fighting for goals and dreams only with our natural styles. We think that all we aspire to be requires only our gifts and talents, and that is precisely where we err.

The inclination of one's thoughts determines the direction of one's path. Before we go off in search of the way, we must first determine our desired end. *Nothing will ever happen until we have the courage to begin. Courage is the key to starting the journey, but wisdom is the light that can show us the way. Without courage you cannot begin, but without wisdom you cannot reach the end.*

That's what "the bridge" is about: crossing the threshold of our dreams with wisdom as our guide. *May our footprints not only take us to our destiny, but may they also forge a trail for others to follow.*

When we think about our lives, our dreams and our desires, let us be courageous enough to dream big. Let us dream about reaching the highest mountaintops, where mere talent cannot take us. Let us dream of those places our hearts long for because only when we dream of them will we know what bridges we need to cross.

Introduction

Don't let the ghosts of past defeat keep you from walking toward your dreams. You may have faced setbacks in the past, and surely you will meet them again in the future, but *with courage at your side* and wisdom as your guide, you will reach new heights.

Choose a life that challenges the possibilities and turns them into realities. Choose to fight great battles to reach great dreams. Choose the strategy that will get you to your destiny. There are places in life that we reach with mere talent, but *maintaining it requires planning for it.* From the bottom of the mountain we behold the summit in all of its glory, but it's one thing to climb it and another to endure it. Otherwise, when you reach the peak, you may come to see that the climb was not the hardest part. You must now find a way to survive. Crossing the bridge of possibilities to the side of realities requires a strategy. It can be done, but you have to know where to start. Success in the pursuit of one's destiny lies in discerning what path to follow. You must know not only what is desired, but also what is required.

I need to know the proper steps to reach my desired end. I need to anticipate that I might fall, but I also need to believe that I will stand up strong. Each step forward takes me closer to my destiny. Though I may not see anything around me, everything I need is inside me, and if I plan my footsteps, my eyes will behold the place for which my soul yearns. We must believe that within us dwells everything we need to cross over the bridge. All we need now are the right strategies to win the battles to come.

Every person has the capacity to choose what kind of life to live. Perhaps we do not choose the starting point, but we all can choose the dream to pursue and the end we wish to ensure.

NEVER GO TO WAR WITHOUT A STRATEGY

I frequently encounter companies and people who have set goals—some are small, and some are big. What surprises me the most is that we are capable of setting goals, but we have a hard time establishing strategies to reach them. It is very much like choosing a destiny and waiting with our arms crossed instead of moving along. If you know where you intend to go, you also need to plan how to get there. You cannot reach a place by merely thinking of it; you need to walk toward it.

Strategy is the fastest vehicle to results. Many of us know the goals we want to reach, but we lack the strategy to reach them, and that is why we never see the results we hope for. Our minds dream of the ideal, but our lives settle for the real, not realizing that *having a strategy could mean the difference between living in the real and making our ideal real.* No matter what your goal may be in life, it takes strategy to achieve it.

Life is a constant battle for what we desire. Do not grow weary of fighting. *Your dreams deserve that you fight for them with everything you have* because you deserve to live life to the fullest and enjoy each moment, in spite of what may come your way. *Your destiny is waiting for you to find your way to it.*

I finished writing this book during the quarantine of COVID-19. A few weeks previously, my friend Erwin McManus had sent me a message asking me how I was doing. His final words were so inspiring that I want to echo them for everyone who navigates these pages.

The message said: "Everyone around the world is in crisis, but we are going to come out of this stronger than we have ever been before. Meanwhile, let us keep moving forward."

I hope that as you read *The Bridge*, you come out stronger on the other side and ready to face new challenges on your way toward new destinies. In these pages, you will find steps to help you reach your desired end. If you have not determined that destination yet, they will help you establish it. My sincere intention is that when you finish reading this book, you will be adequately prepared with a strategy that allows you to reach the place to which your mind aspires and your heart desires.

STRATEGY IS WHERE I GIVE MY
GOALS, MY LONGINGS AND MY
DREAMS THE OPPORTUNITY
TO COME ALIVE.   XAVIER CORNEJO

1

Strategy

"Winning should be owed only to the virtue of strategy. It is sufficient to train in it to be useful at all times, And to teach it for it to be useful in all things. This is how the true way of strategy must be."

—MIYAMOTO MUSASHI

"We all live under the same sky, but we don't all have the same horizon," observed Konrad Adenauer.[3] Some words are never forgotten; they carve their way into our minds and into our hearts. These words did precisely that for me. We all live under the same sky, and we all have the same opportunities to breathe, to reach and to achieve, but at the same time, we all see different places, we have different goals, different dreams, and that's what makes every life so important.

Because only you can be you, only you can dream something I wouldn't even dare to imagine.

---

3   First Chancellor of the Federal Republic of Germany (West Germany) from 1949 to 1963.

I am convinced that inside every one of us there are gifts, talents and abilities. Some may have already found them, but many are still looking to find theirs. Whether you have discovered them or not, I am convinced that we all have goals we seek to attain and experiences we desire to gain. Ultimately, we all want to know which path will lead us to that realm.

STRATEGIES ARE DESIGNED TO WIN

Maybe you wish to write a book, start a business or double your sales. Perhaps you aspire to be a famous actor or actress, an eloquent public speaker or an inspiring figure. No matter how small the goal may seem or how big and complex it turns out to be, the question is always the same: What is your strategy?

In order to win a war, a strategy must reign and roar. No army goes to war without a strategy.

A chess master cannot win the game without a defined strategy. He observes his opponent slowly, while quickly thinking through his next moves.

Businessmen advance and succeed according to their strategies.

Every doctor forms a strategy to heal a patient.

Great Olympic athletes don't win by talent alone. They do it by strategizing because the line that separates them from their competitors is practically invisible.

Therefore, if you want victory, you must develop a strategy. Your strategy must be designed carefully and evaluated constantly. It must be coupled with thorough analysis and an action plan. Different results are not achieved randomly, rather with daily consistency.

I like to reminisce of summer days and nights once upon a time when I would play with my cousins, Antonio and Gaby. We would go to their house in Machángara and play board games all night. Whether it was Monopoly or Bon Voyage, from the moment we threw the dice, we would be mentally developing a strategy that would lead us to victory.

If you have ever played a board game or any card game, you know what I'm talking about. From the beginning of the game, you are already thinking about what strategy to use, the spaces you would like to land on or the places you should buy.

It amazes me that even though we all have the ability to develop strategies to win in a board game, we do not use that same ability to win the most important game of them all—the game of life. If winning a board game is important to us, how much more important should it be to have a strategy to reach our dreams. In life, we must be like a war strategist whose greatest objective is winning the battle and building the bridge that leads to success.

It's time to think about the strategies to win the war and reach our goals. Our future hangs on our decisions and our actions. The result of strategy is not a matter of failure and success. It is a matter of life or death. Strategy is where I give my goals, my longings and my dreams the opportunity to come alive.

One of life's greatest battles is keeping our capacity to dream big alive, and we must do so with every beat of our heart and every breath from our lungs. The end goal of strategy should be to conquer and enjoy everything for which our soul longs. With the passing of time, we realize that we should have been wiser with the way we spent our days. Though the years may have slipped away, there is still time for dreams to be fulfilled. As long as there is breath in your lungs, every battle for your dreams can be won.

Life is a battlefield between what we want and what we don't want, between what we desire and what we fear, between enduring or quitting, and between staying in the possibility or crossing the bridge to a better reality. To win that battle, you need a strategy that will take you farther toward your destiny and lead you over the bridge.

INTELLIGENCE FOR THE STRATEGY

Strategy is merely thought-out steps to cross over the bridge to your desired destination. Often, we walk through life focused on goals we aim to reach and dreams we long to fulfill, not knowing what steps can take us to that place. We tend to think that in order to achieve greatness, we need to work harder. I am convinced that hard work does not always lead us on the paths that we imagine or to the destinies to which we aspire.

I know a lot of people who worked hard just so their eyes could behold tomorrow, but now their vision is one of sorrow. Working hard is an essential part of reaching a goal, but working smart is the key ingredient to reaching the other side.

BEGIN BY THINKING

How much time do we truly invest in thinking about how to reach our goals? If our thought patterns dictate our feet's rhythm, could it be that we have not crossed over to the other side because we have worked hard to get there, but not thought enough about how to get there?

Many of us have thought about losing weight or increasing our economy. I find it interesting that we often choose to exercise heavily instead of eating cleverly. We fail to notice that, though exercise is important, nutrition is far more important to reaching our goal.

Proven by countless research studies, the formula to lose weight is 80 percent diet and 20 percent exercise. However, when you are over-weight by more than 30 pounds, the ratio correspondingly changes to 90/10. Usually, when one reaches the ideal weight, a 50/50 ratio is recommended.[4]

We can follow endless formulas, but we will always need a thought-out strategy to reach our much-sought-after goal. Additionally, if I want to lose two pounds, the strategy will be different than if I want to lose 50 pounds.

If we are concerned about having more money, the first thing we may think about is how to earn more money, instead of how to spend less money. If both things can be done, the more beneficial the outcome. But strategy will always be based on the goal I desire to reach and what my thought patterns need to be for my ambition to be within my

---

4 "What is the ideal ratio of diet versus exercise?" *Body Knows Best.* Oct. 24, 2018. http://bodyknowsbest.net/ideal-ratio-of-diet-vs-exercise/.

reach. Similarly, if I wish to save $1,000, the strategy will differ from wanting to save $20,000.

BEHOLD WHERE YOU ARE TO GET TO WHERE YOU ARE GOING

Has it ever crossed your mind that the importance of a GPS is not only its capacity to show your destination and how to get there, but also its ability to know where you are? The GPS would not be able to guide us without first determining where we are. Its satellites and receptors need first to determine where you are before it can calculate the distance to the place you are headed.

No matter where you are headed, where you are is essential in relation to your destination. Whether you're near or far is not relevant; what matters most is knowing where you are currently. That is where you will choose the path you should follow.

This reminds me of the words of Sun Tzu: "If you know the enemy and know yourself, you need not fear the result of a hundred battles. If you know yourself but not the enemy, for every victory gained you will also suffer a defeat." That is the importance of knowing where you are in relation to where you are headed. If you know what you aim for and where the path begins, you will be able to plan how to reach each and every dream.

We don't have a GPS for the journey of life. That is precisely why we need a strategy to serve as our guide. Having a strategy motivates us to not only embark on the journey, but also to enjoy it.

A strategy must be designed to reach the other side, but it must be developed from where I am today. Only when we know where we are will we be able to understand how much time it will take to cross the bridge to the land where opportunities can transform into realities.

Some people become discouraged because they never calculated the time it would take for their dreams to unfold. While there are small goals that are important, other goals will take our whole life and require consistency and persistence.

STRATEGY TRACES THE ROUTE

I recently met up with my cousin, Fausto, who spent a few days vacationing with his family on a cruise. We had the opportunity to have lunch together. While we walked through Brickell City Centre in Miami, Florida, I asked him a few questions about his job. He had previously managed a successful company, but then he went on to work for a company that was struggling. He was able to help it recover and move forward.

I asked him how he brought about that change, and he gave me the following answer: "Strategy." I asked him a couple more questions, specifically which was the first step, and he responded: "I had to first analyze where the company was and the status of each of its parts. Once you have the internal knowledge, you can establish the external strategies." Before knowing where you want to go, you must know where you are. A well thought-out strategy is one that begins with recognizing where you are.

Never fear where you are today; fear not knowing where you want to go tomorrow. Life may have taken you down; you may even feel forsaken, but the important thing is that you still have not been overtaken. As long you are able to stand up, you will have the opportunity to fight back. Only this time around, you have the opportunity to think more clearly about where you are headed.

PREPARE YOUR STRATEGY WITH BOLDNESS AND COURAGE

Fear is the greatest thief that resides in our minds. "Fear doesn't stop death, it stops life," said Elisabeth Kübler-Ross, a pioneer in near-death studies.[5] Fear, if you allow it, will steal your dreams, your future and will make you doubt you could ever achieve everything that you believe. It will lead you to think that what others may say is far more important than where you aim.

However, God created you to dream. He created you to imagine. He has the best future in mind for you. Most of all, don't worry about what others say because they are not part of your story, and they will be amazed to see you reach the glory.

I am certain the best weapon a person can carry is courage: the courage to pursue the life they desire, to conquer the dreams they imagine. Fear of failure, of missing the mark, the shame of what others could say, can take hold of our minds. I've found that what the heart wants scares the mind.

---

5   Swiss-American Psychologist, most respected authority in investigations about death and the dying process, and author of the internationally successful seller *On Grief and Grieving*, 2007.

Fear can lead us to failure before we even step out, but courage can lead us to victory if we step in. We just need to advance. May our courage to step out toward a new future be greater than the voices that tie us to the same past!

I think that what we call a comfort zone is nothing more than the limits of our courage. Therefore, if we never dare cross the frontiers of the things we fear, how will we ever cross the bridge to the other side where our happiness resides? With the virtue of strategy we can draw the path toward victory. While strategy does not bury fear, it does multiply courage.

CIRCUMSTANCES WILL SURROUND YOU BUT STRATEGY WILL GROUND YOU

Although there are circumstances we cannot control, we can control our thoughts, our work and our walk. I like Albert Einstein's words: "It's not that I'm so smart, it's just that I stay in problems longer." I invite you to think about the following: Could the reason you have not reached all that you have envisioned be that you have not thought out a plan to get there? Every human being has the capacity to think, dream, embrace life and to improve each day, but, above all, the ability to pursue their dreams. There is no limit to what you can achieve or the battles that you can win when strategizing is in your mindset.

How I think about my goals is far more important than the goals themselves because how I think of them should propel me forward and toward them instead of toward making excuses of how I may never reach them.

Thinking deeper into the details is the key that opens the door to a better tomorrow. No matter the resources you have at hand, you can always increase the resources you have in your head. What you lack will never be a good excuse not to fight for what you want. The reason many of us don't put our thoughts to work is because we've bought into the lie that our thoughts are not worth much, that we are not smart enough to get to where we've always dreamed of.

I want you to know that your thinking is what leads you to your triumphs—or your failures. How people think determines how they behave and the final outcome that surrounds them. This is as true for people as it is for any organization. Beyond the difficulty of our goals lies the quality of our thoughts.

The only things that are certain are the sunsets we have lived and the stories we have told. No one on earth has a guaranteed new sunrise, but the beauty of life is found in what tomorrow may bring. Tomorrow is a place full of possibilities. Embrace them! Any step in my day can lead me across the bridge to where my dreams abide and my goals reside.

The pursuit of something better, of something greater, should always be in our minds and within sight. If we cannot imagine a better tomorrow, we will insist on holding onto a past that no longer exists. There is a saying: "To remember is to live again." But remembering does not move me into the future and is not a substitute for flying. The best flight is the one that takes me to the tomorrow I long for.

We think that a second is nothing, but life slips away second by second; minute by minute it fades, and day by day it evaporates. At the end of the day, each second you let get away is a second that will not come back your way. Every second you fail to pursue what you desire is a moment of life wasted in something that is not required.

EVERY GREAT VISION REQUIRES A STRATEGY FOR ITS FRUITION

In May 2019, my friend Emerson invited me to participate in a conference that took place in Mexico City, Mexico. He has an incredible story, and he is a leader whom I admire deeply. At that time, it had been a year since he had moved from Los Angeles, California, to Mexico City, along with his wife, Cristina, and son Lincoln, to start Mosaic Mexico.

After only a few months of being there, he organized a conference with an attendance of about 600 people, and I had the opportunity to be there. A year later, Mosaic organized a conference with a higher attendance, in a venue with greater capacity. With higher vision came greater risks, but he who avoids risks avoids opportunities. This time, the place had the capacity to sit 1,200 people, and the attendance exceeded all expectations.

When we had a break in the middle of the conference, as we walked over to a restaurant, we had the opportunity to talk. He told me how difficult it had been to organize this conference in comparison to the previous one. Of course, it was a great achievement: He had doubled attendance in less than 12 months! When I asked him what the difference was between the first and second conference, his words were, "It took a lot more strategy." Every great vision requires a strategy to reach fruition. The fastest way to double results is not through talent; it is through strategy. Every outcome is on the other side of a bridge crossed, a strategy traced with a clear mind and a life aimed to reach the desired end.

The Chess Grandmaster Gary Kasparov played 2,400 chess games and only lost 170 times. That's less than 10 percent of his professional career. If anyone knows about strategy, they're the chess grandmasters. In his book *Deep Thinking*, Gary Kasparov writes, "By 1985, computers were already powerful enough to compute every possible combination of moves over the next three or four turns and pick the most appropriate one. But, if the player was able to strategize at least five moves ahead, it was quite possible for him to defeat a computer."[6] Just as strategy is necessary in chess, it is also necessary in life. The more your strategy evolves, the farther you can go and the stronger enemies you can overthrow. Nowadays, computers are far more powerful and advanced and have the capacity to constantly beat the grandmasters of chess. Just as computers have become more powerful enemies, life has become more challenging for us. Even when we live in a time where resources abound, difficulties also overflow.

From now on, when you think about the future, think of how you will get there and what strategy you will use. The greatest challenge in reaching a goal is not its complexity but rather your mentality. Thinking can be exhausting, but not thinking can be devastating. If

---

6   Kasparov, Gary Kimovitch, and Mig Greengard. *Deep Thinking: Where Machine Intelligence Ends and Human Creativity Begins*. John Murray Publishers, 2018.

you could trace the course to the other side, which steps would you need to keep in mind? At the end, strategy is nothing more than the path I choose to reach my vision—the steps I envision to achieve my mission.

YOUR STRATEGY CAN CHANGE ALONG THE WAY

In the movie I mentioned at the beginning of this book, *Creed II*, many things inspire me, but one of the most influential perspectives I adopted for myself is this: In the beginning, Creed decided to face Drago, and this fight became his biggest dream.

After preparing himself arduously, he went to battle. He was defeated with no mercy by a seemingly invincible giant. Later in the movie, he faced the same opponent but was able to defeat him. What had changed? Had his dream changed? No. He did not change his dream; he changed his strategy!

It's possible that the only reason we cannot turn our possibilities into realities is because we have not changed our strategies. If it's a matter of strategy, why is changing so difficult for us? Truth be told, it is our mentality that we need to change. It's not always the strategy I envisioned for myself that is the most beneficial. In the case of the movie, the strategy that helped Adonis Creed to win was the strategy Rocky planned for him.

The best ideas for me do not always come from me. Allow yourself to expand the way you think. Perhaps the key that opens the door to your destiny resides in someone else's mind, and maybe, the key that can open someone else's future is in your mind.

Creed's victory, aided by Rocky's strategy, made me think that, sometimes, the people who are close to us and on our side are the ones who are able to see certain things in our dreams and strategies—things we fail to see due to our eagerness to reach what we seek.

To create a strategy, we need to carry out things to get across and reach the other side. In the pages to come you will find thoughts that can help you design strategies to reach any goal you may have in mind.

My deepest desire for you is that, after reading this book, you develop a strategy that you can employ and deploy to unfold your dreams and enjoy your life. May you cross over the bridge and turn possibilities into realities.

OPEN YOUR MIND TO THE POSSIBILITY THAT IMPOSSIBILITY IS ATTAINABLE

I love to talk with my son, Lucas. In his mind, everything is possible; his reasoning on things surprises me. Every morning we play Roblox (a computer game for different platforms). He plays on his iPad, and I play on my phone. We each have our own characters, and we face off in different worlds of virtual adventures.

Sometimes we have to find treasures or reach certain goals, and his reasoning of how to attain them is unusual for me. Though I often doubt whether I should follow him, he has led us to the treasures on more than one occasion. His childlike mentality beats my adult-like rationality.

Strategy

I believe that occasionally, to obtain the treasure we seek, we must leave all logic of what we deem possible and open our minds to the possibility that the impossible can be obtainable.

Changing your strategy also requires the courage to try methods you've never tried before.

One of the greatest expressions of courage is to believe so strongly in your destiny that fear to fail cannot derail you. It is in failure that we learn life's greatest lessons that allow us to adjust our steps. If we never fail, instead of flight we may experience only plight.

One of the books I have enjoyed reading is a book by Laura Teme titled *Become a Success by Failing*. It is in failure that I acquire the necessary ingredients to attain success. Allow yourself to fail because that is the best way to improve.

You need to become a grandmaster of strategy because life, though beautiful, is rapidly fleeting. Suddenly, we find ourselves at the end of the way wishing for everything we could have attained every day.

Be courageous in the search of your life. Be courageous to write your story. Be courageous in the pursuit of your dreams—no matter the obstacles you run into along the way or the opinions that are tossed your way. When you reach the end of your days, only you will be held accountable for what you did with each new day.

To create a strategy is to believe that everything can be achieved.

REFLECTION QUESTIONS

1. Are my dreams important enough to fight for them?

   _____

   _____

2. Am I aware that by developing a strategy, I am giving my dreams and goals a chance to come alive?

   _____

   _____

3. What strategies do I need to design in order to achieve my dreams or goals?

   _____

   _____

4. Where am I in relation to my goals?

   _____

   _____

5. What steps must I have in mind to cross the bridge from possibility to reality?

   _____

   _____

CLARITY IS THE AIR I NEED TO BREATHE TO REACH THE MOUNTAIN PEAK.

XAVIER CORNEJO

2

Clarity

Where do I want to go, and how will I get there?

This question has brought the most clarity into my life. One of the main reasons we do not accomplish what we dream is because our dreams are not clear. Most of us know that we want something better, but we lack the capacity to describe it with clarity.

"You cannot go to a place in reality that you haven't first visited in your imagination." When I heard my friend and mentor, Dr. Dale Bronner, say this, my mind took flight. Imagination invites us to dream, and it also highlights the bridge.

I was at a conference in Atlanta called "Re-imagine," and one of the speakers quoted this great truth from I. V. Hilliard: "The power to define is the power to determine destiny." Taking the time to define what you want eliminates the detours you don't want.

Planning clearly is the result of thinking cleverly. Clarity is the light that defies and defines our path. It's the lighthouse that illuminates our track. As Anne Frank used to say, "Look at how a single candle can both defy and define the darkness."

Decisions determine destiny. When I don't know where I'm going, any path will take me there. The best decisions I can make are the ones that lead to the place I deeply long to reach. If I don't know where I'm headed, I may get lost in the landscape without ever reaching the end of my journey.

A bridge is a point of connection between two places—between two destinies. It's the place that connects who I am with who I want to be and what I want to do. I need clarity to cross the bridge to the side where my dreams awake and my goals await. I need to know precisely where I want to go to know exactly which bridge I ought to cross.

Several months ago, I was at author Sonia Luna's offices. They, and everything she and her husband have built, are fascinating. I am convinced that only bright minds that surround themselves with brilliant teams can achieve what they have achieved. One of the things I learned during my time there was about the intentional use of lighting. They explained that, through their lighting methods, they mark the path that people must follow to get to where they need to go. The light intensity marks the path people must follow.

That is clarity: It's the light that illuminates my track, if it is success I want to find in my path. Defining with clarity is turning on the light where my feet can walk; it's the air I need to breathe to reach the mountain peak. Clarity allows me to develop a better strategy. It helps me be intentional with my steps by giving me ideas on how to obtain my goals—for only then can I see where to step

WHEN THE SKIES ARE CLEAR THE PEAKS APPEAR

Horizons can be appreciated in fullness when the skies are the clearest. Clarity clears the clouds that keep me from imagining my future.

In Ecuador, there is a road that takes you from Cuenca to Guayaquil. It has some of the most beautiful scenery I have ever enjoyed. At the beginning of the drive, you go through El Cajas National Park, a beautiful place filled with lakes. Each scene is more beautiful than the one before. It takes my breath away and invites me to dream awake.

On that road from the mountains to the coast, when the skies are clear, you can see the Chimborazo, an inactive volcano 20,564 feet in height. Not only that, but the peak of the Chimborazo is also the farthest point on the planet from the center of the earth. To behold this wonder from that road is only possible when the skies are clear.

The same happens with a goal; when clouds don't interfere, thinking is clear, and the peak of that beautiful mountain seems near.

When clouds dissipate, mountaintops emanate. Clarity opens our understanding; it shows us where we are standing. Clarity can highlight your destiny.

One of the reasons we don't reach the place we desire is because we lack the clarity to define it. Lack of clarity clouds my inspiration and limits my imagination. It stops my pace by keeping me at base.

CLARITY SHOWS US THE WAY

The launch of my first book, *La historia dentro de ti* (*The Story Within You*), took place in Cuenca, the beautiful city in Ecuador where I was born. During my visit there, I had the opportunity to meet with my cousin Francisco for a few hours. He has a fascinating story that speaks about the power of clarity and our desire to get to where we aspire.

In 2015, Francisco went to Australia with his wife Daniela and their sons Juan Daniel and Tomás—then three and one—to study abroad. At the time, he had an excellent job as the VP of Marketing in a company recognized worldwide.

However, he had clarity regarding what he wanted: to get a master's degree to further his career. He had received a scholarship, and he could choose from the best universities in the world. After looking at all of his options closely, he decided to study in Melbourne, Australia, probably the farthest place from Cuenca, Ecuador.

His clarity concerning what he wanted to achieve helped him decide which path to take, and more importantly, it gave him both the courage to go and the wings to fly. *That's the role of clarity: not only to illuminate the destination in mind and show us the path, but also to give us the courage to fly.* His story is inspiring. He had much to overcome and had to fight for his family to thrive. I'm sure one day he will write that story.

Not only did he graduate with honors with his master's degree in communication, but he also launched his digital marketing agency, which works with various distinguished brands. Along with his wife Daniela (who had the idea), they developed an app that helps parents to better connect with their kids.

The app is called *Storybook*.[7] As I finish writing this book, it already has more than one million downloads. It combines the benefits of infant massage with storytelling to help children relax and sleep better, in addition to other psychological and emotional benefits. Above all, it encourages parents and their children to connect through quality time and touch.

That is why, when he invited me to his house to show me digital marketing tools, how they work and strategies that I could take advantage of, I could not turn down his invitation. While I was there, he asked if I had already thought about the audience for my book.

Furthermore, he told me that the best way to know the most effective strategy to promote my book would come from thinking about the people who would read it: their work, their education, their likes and dislikes, they locations and their ages. He told me I should imagine it with so much detail as to even give names to the people. Only then

---

7   http://storybook-app.com

would I have the clarity that I needed. He told me this concept is called "buyer persona." People who are just starting their business endeavors, or who don't want or cannot afford to spend a lot of money in market research, use this method before jumping into the void. This way they can determine which strategy to use and where to promote so their budgets can be used more efficiently. He explained that by doing this, the abstract becomes tangible, and we can go from what's general to something specific and concrete.

That's what clarity is all about: being able to see the goal concretely. Many of us have goals—things we want to achieve—but can we describe them concretely, or are they in our mind as abstract ideas yet to be defined?

We often waste days, months and years simply due to the lack of clarity regarding what we truly desire. We talk in abstract ways instead of absolutes. We say things like, "I want to lose weight," and we leave it at that without ever defining the goal further.

Defining what you want gives you the power to pursue it, but more importantly, it gives you the strength to achieve it. If you cannot see clearly, you will never chase your dream correctly because you will never know which bridge to cross to reach your goal.

I have heard it said that a well-defined problem is a half-solved problem. I would love to say the same is true of our goals. Though defining the goal with clarity doesn't mean you have it half achieved, it is the starting point to making possible what seems impossible.

Clarity

One night, I was listening to an inspiring interview that Erwin McManus was doing with Jerry Lorenzo (founder and designer of one of my favorite brands, Fear of God). They were talking about creativity in times of crisis, and one of the most interesting concepts that Jerry shared was this: "When the vision is clear, decisions are easy." When you know exactly where you want to go, you know what road to take, and you recognize which bridge you must not miss."

In the same interview, Erwin concluded by saying, "The most powerful thing you can have is a clear image of the future that God wants you to build." It's not enough to have a vague image. The power lies in having a clear image. *We should have clarity from the start of the race to know which route to embrace.* Clarity defines the path to take to reach the desired end.

REFLECTION QUESTIONS

1. Where do I want to arrive?

2. Can I define clearly what I want to achieve?

3. Can I be more specific than I was in the answers to the previous two questions?

4. Now that I know where I want to go, what decisions should I make?

5. Since I have a clear goal in mind, can I see which bridge I need to cross?

UNITY GIVES RISE TO LOYALTY.

XAVIER CORNEJO

3

People

*"Imagine what it would be like if tigers could learn
how to move together—if tigers would choose to stand
side by side and engage in battle as one tribe."*

—ERWIN RAPHAEL MCMANUS

An old adage advises, "If you want to go fast, go alone, but if you want to go far, go together." Though I like how it sounds and I understand its meaning, I do not agree with it. In my opinion, *the fastest way to cross the bridge is with company.* Crossing the bridge to our goals and dreams requires that people walk with us, pull us up when we fall and encourage us when we lack the strength to go on. There will be times when others lift us and times when we will lift others.

There is beauty in knowing that, though there are people who wish for us to fail, there are many more who wish for us to gain. Perhaps you can win a small battle alone, but *to win a war, you need an army.*

THE BRIDGE

Armies don't win wars simply because of their large numbers of soldiers. They win wars because of what each soldier contributes to the whole—their ability in solidarity with their brothers in arms. Soldiers provide their talents and unique mentality to help execute the winning strategy. Unity gives rise to loyalty. Before someone can fight for you and by your side, there must be unity, friendship and loyalty. Before stepping onto the battlefield, the two of you must become brothers and sisters, united by a bond stronger than blood.

It doesn't happen frequently, but one time I woke up in the middle of the night with a single thought racing through my mind, burning in my heart. This principle has opened many doors and helped me cross many bridges: *In order to run together toward a dream, we must first walk together toward a mission.*

This taught me that in order to advance toward our dreams, we need people who can walk with us toward our mission, but we must also be willing to walk with them toward theirs. I am convinced that at the end of the path, both our missions will converge together as one, in a place we call fulfilled dreams.

For that reason, it wasn't much of a surprise when I came across these lines in the book *Activate Your Brain* by Scott G. Halford[8]:

> Several studies have shown that we're smarter when we're with others. Teams achieve better results than any solo expert on a given topic. Clearly, we should try to collaborate more with others.

---

8   Halford, Scott G. *Activate Your Brain: How Understanding Your Brain Can Improve Your Work—and Your Life.* Greenleaf Book Group Press, 2015.

Working with others shouldn't be a chore, though, since it increases not only our productivity, but gives us joy, too.

By reaching a goal with others, we feel more joy and happiness than if we had gotten there alone, and this is because with others our oxytocin levels rise. Shared joy is magnified joy.

From some studies we know that *coactive working*—meaning working in the same office on independent projects and sharing information—increases happiness and productiveness. The *best* results, however, are achieved through *interactive working*, that is, people working together toward a common goal.

It doesn't matter if the objective is personal or organizational. In both cases, you need an army: loyal people who are willing to fight for you and for whom you are willing to fight and give your life.

There is no greater bond than the willingness to sacrifice your life so that others can achieve their dreams. Additionally, the best gift someone can give you is their willingness to give their life so you can reach your dreams. This reminds me of the words of Edwin Louis Cole: "Heroes are men who act in a moment in time on a need greater than they are."

The measure of your life will be evaluated by the number of people you helped on your way up. If, at the end of your days, you reached the other side alone, you will have wasted your life. Joy comes from sharing your life. Sadness oftentimes is nothing more than your soul longing for someone with whom to share life.

THE BRIDGE

It's important to clarify that walking in unity does not mean that there will be no disagreements. To a certain extent, conflict can enhance our way of thinking because we tend to believe that the only valid point of view is our own. Disagreements help us see what others see. That doesn't mean that your point of view is wrong; it means that your ability to see and understand needs to grow.

There is always something new to know, and that knowledge helps us grow. It should be noted that, though there will be disagreements along the way, there must be no disagreements in the location of our destination. When there are disagreements in the location of the destination, perhaps it's time for each person to embark on their own journey.

Find someone with whom to walk in life and share every step of the journey because, on the way to our big dreams, we will often feel tired and frustrated. At those times, the people who surround us can encourage and strengthen us. Those who believe in us are treasures we must value. We speed up the rhythm to our dreams when we are the strength someone else can lean on so they can go on.

Many people don't know where to find such a treasure. Unfortunately, the main reason is that they themselves have not become a treasure for someone else. *Your worth does not increase with what you get; it increases with what you give.* You will neither reach your dreams nor write a big story if all you think about is how you are going to win in this relationship.

IF YOU CAN CROSS THE BRIDGE ALONE YOUR DREAMS ARE FAR TOO SMALL

Great dreams are reached with great friends who walk at our side. With this thought in mind, Walter Isaacson writes in his book *The Innovators*[9]:

> Pop culture portrays genius as being the domain of "lone wolves," who make great discoveries by shutting out the world and immersing themselves in theories and wild experiments. While romantic, this myth is not really how innovation comes about. Innovation instead is a child of collaboration. Even the most introverted innovators were encouraged and nurtured by a circle of friends and creative minds, helping them toward the discoveries that ensured their lasting legacies.

The book, aside from mentioning Steve Jobs and Bill Gates, talks about Ada Lovelace, Lord Byron's daughter, a pioneer in computer programming in the 1840s, and other extraordinary people who paved the way to the digital revolution that surrounds us: Larry Page, cofounder of Google; Robert Noyce, "the Mayor of Silicon Valley," cofounder of Intel and creator of the microchip; Tim Berners-Lee, inventor of the World Wide Web, and many others.

PEOPLE CONNECT US TO THE FUTURE

We also need guides who can show us the path: people who believe in us and have walked before us. It's necessary always to have people to whom we can look up. *Never assume you know it all because that is*

---

9   Isaacson, Walter. *The Innovators: How a Group of Hackers, Geniuses, and Geeks Created the Digital Revolution.* Simon & Schuster, 2015.

the beginning of knowing nothing at all. If you have clarity of where you want to land, you will have clarity regarding whom *you need at your side.*

People often open doors for us, though it is up to us to walk through them. Not many people know the story of how I ended up at Whitaker House. It's not a secret; it's simply not something I get asked a lot. However, the answer to how someone from Cuenca, Ecuador, ended up as the director of the Spanish division of a publishing house based in Pittsburgh, Pennsylvania, is people!

Joann Webster is the name of the person who opened the door for me to be at Whitaker House. I met Joann through her brother Paul Cole. The connections go even farther back, but I'll start the story there. Joann ran a publishing company called *Watercolor Books*, which published books by well-known author Edwin Louis Cole.

When I started publishing books in Ecuador, I decided to visit Joann to understand her vision better and seek new opportunities. To my surprise—because she is a very busy person—Joann made some time in her schedule for me, and we talked for hours. She became my mentor on how the publishing world works. At that time, I felt as if she knew everything, and I knew nothing. She was very kind to teach me how the industry worked.

I worked with Joann for many years until one day, I received a call from her to let me know that Edwin Louis Cole's books would now be published by Whitaker House, including several Spanish titles. She paused for a few seconds, and then she said the following: "Whitaker House is looking for someone who can help them with Spanish books.

Bob asked me if I knew anyone, and I told him yes." Then she added, "I told him that you would be the perfect person for the job."

She told me that there would be a meeting in Pittsburgh in the forthcoming weeks, and I should attend. I went to that meeting, and it ended up being my job interview. That very same day, they told me they wanted me.

It wasn't only my gifts and abilities that connected me with the future; it was the people around me who opened the door.

PEOPLE GIVE US STRATEGIES

In the same way, in the movie *Creed II*, it wasn't Creed who knew how to face that battle; Rocky saw what Creed needed to do to win. People around us can often see what it will take for us to win the battle. Creed had talent, but he lacked the strategy, and even though Rocky provided him with one, Creed had to do the fighting. There are people who can point us in the direction of the bridge, but we are the ones who need to move our feet.

You need to have people you can ask for advice when you don't know how to advance or how to embrace the strategy to expand. We all need someone we can ask for directions, somebody who can teach us how to win. In Joshua's story, it's God who gives him the winning strategy.

No matter what your walk in life is, or what your beliefs are, if your dreams are important, and you don't know which way to go, you can always speak to God. Take a few minutes and ask Him for wisdom for the road ahead so you can be able to reach your dreams someday.

THE BRIDGE

In James 1:5 (NKJV), I find the following words: "If any of you lacks wisdom, you should ask God, who gives generously to all without finding fault, and it will be given to you."

The strategy that led Joshua to triumph was a very unusual one: attack a city protected by walls. Sun Tzu, one of the greatest strategists who ever lived, says the following:

> Maintaining an army is expensive: A host of 100,000 men can cost 1,000 ounces of silver a day for provisions like food, chariots, spears, arrows, armor and oxen. Prolonged warfare can exhaust the resources of any state, leaving it weak and vulnerable.
>
> Hence, aim for quick and decisive victories, not prolonged campaigns. Avoid besieging walled cities, because this usually takes months of preparations, and many impatient generals will squander their men in pointless attacks.[10]

However, Joshua didn't take months of preparation. It only took him seven days to conquer that city because when God is in the equation, there is no goal you cannot reach, no dream you cannot fulfill, no ocean you cannot navigate, no mountain you cannot climb, and no battle you cannot win. *When the wisdom of God is present, everything is different, and nothing is impossible.* To win, you need all the wisdom you can accumulate. Give yourself a chance to win.

---

10 Sun Tzu. *The Art of War*. Westview Press, 1994.

WHO WALKS WITH ME?

Some of the greatest treasures in my life are not only the people who show me the way, but also the brave warriors who have led the way. With the same courage exhibited by those who lead the way, we *must have the courage to walk the way. That is the courage we need to reach our destination.*

Your courage can illuminate your path; your courage can inspire others to walk their paths, too. The most important thing about reaching a dream is not for me to increase, but rather for others to increase due to my dreams.

Therefore, the key question is this: *Who walks with me?* If no one is walking with you, it's probably because you decided not to walk with anybody. *When you are a light for others, others will be a light for you.*

This is another important question: *Who inspires and guides your life?* Whoever inspires you, motivates you, and you motivate those whom you inspire. May you always have a genuine desire to help others, to inspire others, and above all things, to serve others. Only then will you generate the impact you want to create.

One of the greatest teachings I learned from Dr. Dale Bronner[11] is this: Increase follows impact. Increase—in all areas of our lives—follows impact. The more people you impact by what you do, the greater your *intake* will be and the greater your *influence* will be. The more people

---

11 Chand, Samuel R., and Dale C. Bronner. *Planning Your Succession: Preparing for the Future*. Mall Pub., 2008.

you help by what you do, the greater will be what you do. The more people benefit from what you create, the greater what you create will be.

That is why the more people like a song, the more people follow the artist who sings that song. The more people are impacted by what you do, the more influence you will have.

Crossing the bridge to your dreams has everything to do with its impact on the world. I don't know anyone who made an impact on the world by doing things that only benefited themselves. *The greatness of a life is not measured by the height of its achievements but by the depth of its footprints—footprints that others can follow.*

I am convinced that among our greatest legacies we can contribute to the world are not our triumphs but our footprints. The footprints you leave on the path pave the way for others to follow.

Whose footprints are you following? What footprints are you leaving behind? Your life wasn't created only so you could reach your destiny. A great life was created to help others find theirs successfully.

People

REFLECTION QUESTIONS

1. Who do I need to achieve my dream?

2. Who inspires and guides my life?

3. Whom am I willing to fight for? Who is willing to fight for me?

4. Who has information that could help me achieve all that I
    want to achieve?

    _____

    _____

    _____

    _____

5. Who can give me some advice that brings me closer to my
    dreams? Have I asked?

    _____

    _____

    _____

    _____

WHEN IT COMES TO THE BATTLES FOR YOUR GOALS, ANY IDEA CAN BE LIKE A SHARPENED WEAPON

XAVIER CORNEJO

Planning

"Planning, calculating, and comparing armies leads to victory."

—SUN TZU

I was playing with my son Lucas on a Saturday evening. A few days before, he had come up with the idea of drawing imaginary animals on cards made of cardboard. Each animal had a different name and different powers, and we could make them fight each other. He had a white cardboard box in which he carried the animal cards and took them everywhere he went. However, on this particular day, he wanted me to draw my own cards so my animals could compete with his.

If you know me at all, then you know that drawing is on the opposite side of the spectrum of my abilities. Besides drawing, my handwriting is worse than that of a child trying to write his name for the first time. That is why I try to stay as far away as possible from writing anything by hand—much less drawing something. Therefore, I thought of an excuse, and I told him that I lacked the creativity. (I did not want to admit my weakness to my child!)

He looked at me with mischief in his wide blue eyes and said, "Dad, draw whatever comes to mind."

I told him that nothing came to mind.

I thought that was my way out, but then he quickly asked me, "Dad, you write books, right?"

I responded, "Yes."

His immediate response: "Use the same creativity that you use when you write books, except that, instead of writing, draw something!"

Considering his answer, I immediately began to draw my characters. I was surprised at how quickly he thought about a solution. Though drawing and writing are two very different things, he used creativity as the bridge, and he did not allow me to believe that I could not do it out of a lack of creativity. The most surprising thing in all of this was how quickly his mind planned his answer so that I could reach the goal that he had in mind for me.

When we have clarity of the place we want to reach, or what we aim to achieve, and we have the people who can guide us or help us, it is time to begin planning.

For me, planning is nothing more than *focused ideas to reach the desired end*. What steps do I need to take to cross the bridge to what I aim to obtain? What can I do to go from where I am to where I want to go? Questions like these help me focus my mind on solutions—not situations. What other questions lead us to planning?

GENERATE IDEAS IMAGINE AND DREAM

In planning, the most essential part is to generate ideas. When you begin planning, do not discard any idea because you never know where it can take you or how it relates to future ideas. When you begin, simply imagine, think and dream. Suddenly, you will realize how those ideas start to give shape and form to the path or paths that you must follow. I am convinced that there is more than one way that can lead to the bridge to our destiny, which is the main reason you should never discard an idea during planning because that could be the very uncharted idea that leads you to the land you dream of. When it comes to the battles for your goals, any idea can be like a sharpened weapon, and you never know which weapon, which movement or which moment will define the battle.

When you think about your goals, what ideas do you have to reach them all? To generate ideas is to accumulate riches, the kind of richness that helps us reach greatness. Create as many ideas as possible about how to walk and how to cross, what bridges to cross and what bridges to avoid. *Avoiding the wrong bridge is just as important as crossing the right one.*

Once you generate ideas, write them down. When you write them down, you will find wonders hidden within. Sometimes, ideas are like a puzzle; each one is a small piece. However, when you put them all together, and each is in its rightful place, you will be able to appreciate the beautiful landscape that completes the journey.

Connecting ideas you had at one time with ideas from another time can change the equation and lead to a powerful combination. In the same way, connecting your ideas with someone else's ideas can accelerate your momentum to reach your final destination. Ponder ideas, connect ideas and formulate a plan of action based upon them.

To treasure your ideas is one of the best investments you can ever make. Never dismiss the potential of an idea; you never know what you may need to recall. I always write down my ideas as notes in my iPhone, and despite the years, often, the answers I need in my present are found in the thoughts I had in the past.

Today, I want you to think freely, believing everything is possible, that crossing the bridge to your goals is attainable. No idea is impossible. To plan, you need all the ideas you can stock up. In his book, *Alchemy*, Rory Sutherland invites us to think differently—from a different perspective. His book has changed my way of thinking more than once.

He writes, "If we attempt to break out of our rational straitjackets and entertain illogical possibilities, we may just stumble upon our most creative ideas yet. If there were a logical answer to the problem you are trying to solve, you probably would have already found it." Perhaps the answer you are looking for is on the path you are trying so hard to avoid. Sometimes logic can be the limit of greatness.

THINKING WITHOUT LIMITS

Several studies have been done about how many thoughts a person has in a day. According to the National Science Foundation, the average person has somewhere between 12,000 and 60,000 thoughts a day. The problem is that 80 percent of them are negative thoughts, and 95 percent of them are thoughts we repeat from the previous day.[12] Often, those negative thoughts block our mind from devising a plan that will take us to the other side. The good news is that 97 percent of those negative thoughts or concerns are usually unfounded and are the result of a pessimistic, unproven perspective.[13]

Additionally, the Laboratory of Neuro Imaging at the University of Southern California says that we have 48.6 thoughts a minute, with an average of 70,000 thoughts a day.[14] *There is* power *in a well-thought-out plan that exercises your mind and allows your imagination to fly!*

In the story I shared about Lucas, he knew the goal he had in mind for me. His mind formulated a plan that I could follow, and I would be able to draw successfully. His plan was simple: "Use the same creativity you use to write books." When you think about your goals, what plans can you employ? What creative methods do you use elsewhere that can help you reach your objectives?

---

12 Galloza, Stephen. "80% Of Thoughts Are Negative...95% Are Repetitive." *The Miracle Zone*, Apr. 30, 2012, http://faithhopeandpsychology.wordpress.com/2012/03/02/80-of-thoughts-are-negative-95-are-repetitive/.

13 Antanaityte, Neringa. "Mind Matters: How to Effortlessly Have More Positive Thoughts." *TLEX Institute*, http://tlexinstitute.com/how-to-effortlessly-have-more-positive-thoughts/.

14 "How Many Thoughts Do We Have Per Minute?" *Reference.com*, https://www.reference.com/world-view/many-thoughts-per-minute-cb7fcf22ebbf8466.

To formulate a plan, we must gather our thoughts, plot the route and pace our stride. *No one goes to battle without first thinking of which weapons to* deploy *or what strategy to* employ. Otherwise, at the end of the road, you would not encounter a war; you would encounter a massacre. We should approach the future in the same way. *The fight for your deepest desires deserves to be fought and planned with all your strength and all your might.*

The etymological root of the word "ideas" means "to see." Ideas open our eyes to possibilities so we can formulate a plan and turn it into a reality. *An idea should inspect the past, inspire the present and innovate the future.*

DISCOVER WHERE YOUR IMAGINATION LIGHTS UP

Generating ideas is far better than simply having them. The difference is that an idea appears or disappears in an instant, while the process of generating ideas can be constant. Often, we seek ideas in times of difficulty. Adversity frequently opens the door to creativity, and creativity invites opportunity to come in and take a seat. Why wait for difficulty to ignite our creativity?

Let us be aware that creation can be constant and not just sporadic. We all have spaces or places where our imagination can ascend and our ideas can transcend. We have moments that not only make us feel alive but also teach us how to thrive. There are times to breathe in to gather everything within to win. What have those breath-taking moments been for you? Have you been able to identify what kinds of moments light up your imagination? Being able to identify them will equip you with the proper ideas to reach the other side.

As we were planning the launch of the book *A Woman Who Dreams* by Omayra Font—one of our most successful authors—she told me about that place where she can think and plan, and how she creates it. When a book impacts her, she buys a physical and a digital copy as well as the audiobook. Then, she listens to the audiobook when she goes running. I asked her why she doesn't listen to music when she runs, to which she answered, "Running is one of the moments in my day that I devote to thinking."

That is the space where she comes up with ideas, and she creates that space intentionally to achieve everything her heart dreams of. That is an example of taking advantage of time and recognizing the moments where you can plan your future and develop strategies.

All of us must be able to identify those moments in our life that invite us to dream, inspire us to think and awaken our creativity. For example, in the movie *Midnight in Paris*, Gil Pender, interpreted by Owen Wilson, goes to Paris with his fiancée's family. Gil is writing a novel, but he cannot find the inspiration to finish it until each night he travels in time and meets up with a great artist from a different era: Ernest Hemingway, Pablo Picasso, Gertrude Stein and others. Having conversations with such artists, with the natural inspiration evoked by Paris in the rain and its nostalgic stores, inspires him to write his book.

I love the art of this movie, but the conversations inspire me more. When the movie ends, I am not only ready to write, I am ready to live. It inspires me so much that I find it easy to come up with ideas.

Similarly, I am persuaded that you also have certain movies or books that invite you to dream and leap, moments that inspire you to imagine or music that compels you to create. Be intentional to seek such moments. Think about everything you may need to win the battle for your dreams.

Intentionally aim to create; seek places where your mind can be free to think, dream and imagine. Cultivating moments like these will help you awaken new dreams. When you invest in new ideas, you turn thoughts into possibilities that can turn into realities. Keep inspiration at the center of your mind so the battle can be won.

PLANNING HOW TO FLY

To plan is to think of the action. The problem is that we spend most of our days reacting to what happened instead of planning what we wish to see happen. *Life can be controlled by our reactions, but it can only be guided by our actions.* You cannot cross the bridge accidentally; you must cross the bridge intentionally. *It is better to look forward and plan than to look back and cry.*

In the story I read about Joshua, before marching into war, God gave the Israelites the plan that would lead them to their goal. The entire army would march around the city once for six days, and on the seventh day it would march seven times around the city. On that day, the musicians would sound their trumpets, and when they had heard the call to war, everyone would lift their voices and shout, which would, in turn, make the walls fall. That was their plan; it sounds strange, but it worked!

When you seek a plan to reach your dream, do not dismiss any possibility. Let us not lose time thinking of the ways it may fail. Let us start thinking of the ways it may prevail.

In the movie *Creed II*, for the rematch, Rocky did not change the goal; he changed the plan. This time, they went to a desert to train differently. No one can deny that Creed trained hard the first time, and even so, he lost. However, the next time around, they had the same talent, the same effort, but a different plan; a smarter plan was the difference between winning and losing. *The question is not whether you have the talent to win or not, the question is whether you have the intelligence to develop a better plan.*

Perhaps you think you lack the necessary capital or reserves, but if you have ideas you have everything you need. You may lack the external resources, but you have all the internal resources. These will help you expand the limitations of your knowledge; use them to plan your takeoff.

The greatest treasure a person owns is not a material possession but rather their priceless potential. Your external assets will always be limited, but your internal assets have no limits. What is in your mind can be multiplied; the brain can always be amplified. It is known as the most powerful computer, [15] and the most valuable collateral any person holds.

---

15 Choi, Charles Q. "Human Brain May Be Even More Powerful Computer than Thought." *NBCNews.com*, NBCUniversal News Group, Oct. 30, 2013, www.nbcnews.com/sciencemain/human-brain-may-be-even-more-powerful-computer-thought-8C11497831.

The material is acquired, the intangible is hardwired. It is what we need to realize our dreams. No one can use a lack of resources as an excuse not to reach their dreams. We all have the capacity to plan and think. The great strategist Sun Tzu says the following: "Thus it is that in war the victorious strategist only seeks battle after the victory has been won, whereas he who is destined for defeat first fights and afterwards looks for victory."

Perhaps I am an idealist, but I believe that we must be willing to face any battle when it comes to our goals and dreams. I would rather go to battle for my dreams, though I could possibly fail, than sit on the fringes, hoping they will arrive one day. At the end of my life, *I would rather have fought for what I desired than lament what could have transpired.*

Planning can save us from failure because it allows us to imagine the different landscapes so that we can control our movements. Blindly chasing after our dreams will not help us reach the place we have in mind. He who plans his steps plans his success. The fight for your goals deserves your all, and you must fight with all your soul. If you do so, you will have already won. *It is time to start dreaming. Deem it a possibility, that with the proper strategy you can get to the other side. There are no obstacles you cannot overcome if you put your mind to work and set your ideas to flight.*

I have fought a thousand battles and have probably lost more than I have won. Some I lost because I simply gave up. Others I fought with my all, but even then, I lost because I lacked an adequate winning strategy. Today I can see that perhaps, had I won the wrong battle, I would be farther from the place where I have triumphed. To fully appreciate who I am and where I am today, I needed to fight each fight. Some I learned to appreciate because I won, but I learned the most from the ones I lost. Out of all my defeats, I only regret those in which I simply gave up.

Do not get trapped in the prison of regret; you will struggle to escape. However, if at some point you fall into the trap and it seems impossible to get out, remember the key that opens the door to your freedom is in your hand and in your mind. Sometimes it is hard to find the light, but those are precisely the moments where you must let your mind fly, imagining the future you want.

Opportunities do not get lost in time. Next time around, they will simply take you to a new place, one you never thought of but with potentially the greatest payoff. The journey of life truly does last a lifetime. Even if some opportunities pass you by, it does not mean a better tomorrow will never arrive; it simply means you are on a different path to a faraway land—a land called destiny.

I try not to look back because that is not the direction I am headed. I like to look forward because each day moves me onward; my goals propel me forward. There are no goals in the past, we can only reach them in the future. I am convinced that creating great memories is not only to have a good past, but to have a great future. I do not fight with all my strength and all my might so I can look back and feel proud, but rather to look ahead to a powerful tomorrow.

THE WISDOM IN LISTENING

The true battle we must win is the battle within. As Master Yoda says, "Weapons do not win battles; your mind, powerful it is." Once we win that battle, we will not be afraid to lose or to change, and even less to listen and learn. Once we conquer the world within, it is much easier to face the world outside. When we die to the need to always be right, we learn how to listen to the ideas around us. This is when we get the power to change whatever throws the plan out of alignment.

Often we fail to adapt the strategy we employ in our fight because pride prevents us from seeing there is a better path to winning. If you can incline your ear, you will hear the wisdom others possess, and nothing will stand in your way to success. Kenneth H. Blanchard[16] said, "None of us is as intelligent as all of us." I have also heard leadership guru Sam Chand share the same sentiments.

Only a person who listens carefully and understands completely will be exalted constantly. In life, we do not achieve success due to our ability to speak but rather our ability to listen. There is no limit to what we can achieve when we learn to hear. Listening takes us from what we know to what we need to know.

The truth is wisdom flows from all those times we held our tongue when we felt the urge to explode. Listening expands my ability to understand. The problem is that most of us hear with our ears to formulate a response, and we do not listen to understand with our hearts.

---

16 "A Quote by Kenneth H. Blanchard." *Goodreads.* http://goodreads.com/quotes/56863-none-of-us-is-as-smart-as-all-of-us#:~:text=Quote%20by%20Kenneth%20H.,smart%20as%20all%20of%20us.%E2%80%9D.

Planning

To enjoy what is to come, we need to learn to listen with our hearts and then discern the best plan.

Tomorrow's possibilities are infinite. Ideas can open the door to a world of endless opportunities. Many of us have given a lot of thought to changing the past, but have we given any to how to reach for what is to come? We need to turn those possibilities into realities. If the future is a place of infinite opportunities, then why not take the time to plan for it?

I have learned from Sam Chand that I should try to think of more than two solutions when I need to solve an issue. He even recommends four to five if possible. The reason is that if we think of only two solutions, we will remain within our binary system of thought. Here we will face a good and a not-so-good solution, and we will generally opt for the more appealing one. However, if we do that, we limit the possibilities other solutions can bring, and when it comes to my goals and my life, I do not want to be limited by one idea. I would rather soar on the possibility of a thousand ideas than remain grounded by the limitations of a single one.

When we activate our minds, we can begin to plan. That is where our ideas have a chance, and the victory can be ours; here is where our ideas can be combined. Listening to the world that surrounds us can help us have more and better ideas. In those precise moments, we can forge the path to the bridge we must cross toward where victory can be ours.

REFLECTION QUESTIONS

1. Can I describe at least five ways to get to my destination?

   _____

   _____

2. Have I managed to identify when I feel most inspired, what moments ignite my imagination?

   _____

   _____

3. Am I generating ideas intentionally or just waiting for them to come to my mind?

   _____

   _____

4. Have I disregarded ideas because they seem illogical to me? What if I connect my illogical ideas with my logical ideas?

   _____

   _____

5. What steps should I take to cross the bridge to the place I want to get to?

   _____

   _____

THE LEVEL OF YOUR PREPARATION DETERMINES
THE LEVEL OF YOUR ELEVATION.

XAVIER CORNEJO

Preparation

"A thousand days of training to develop, ten thousand days
of training to polish. You must examine all this well."

—MIYAMOTO MUSASHI

HOW AND FOR WHAT ARE YOU PREPARING YOURSELF?

The cumulative results of our lives—the goals we do or do not achieve,
the destinations to which we do or do not arrive—are the products
of our preparation. *It's better to sweat in practice than to bleed in battle.*
Awards are not earned by sweating the day of the competition; they
are achieved with the sweat of the days of preparation. Your game-day
performance reveals your determination—it's the evidence of the persistence with which you have worked and endured.

For an amateur boxer to make it through three rounds, he has to train
for six rounds.[17] In other words, his preparation requires twice as
much work as the fight itself.

---

17 "How Long Do Boxers Train Before the First Fight?" *Cleto Reyes*. Sept. 17, 2019. http://
cletoreyesshop.com/how-long-do-boxers-train-before-first-fight/.

Fighters typically train between three to five hours a day, five times a week, because they believe the better they prepare, the higher their chances of winning the fight. Their training is not only intense, it's also smart. They educate themselves about their opponents, so they know what to expect from them and, above all, how to approach them.

Boxers in the Top 10 can spend between 15 to 20 years of their lives training, pushing themselves to the limits of their abilities to reach the top levels.[18]

Life is a battle between what you want and what you do not want, between the ideal and the real. It's a battle for what you long for and desire, but in order to achieve it you must prepare yourself to win. In the same way that a boxer trains for his bouts, you have to ready yourself for your battles. Strength is forged with perseverance, and wisdom comes from that very experience. Your goals must be as important to you as these fights are to those boxers.

The number of fights an amateur boxer needs to become a professional can be as diverse as the number of people in the world. Many things play a factor, such as the age at which he began to fight, the country where he resides and others. However, on average, some of the best boxers in history had approximately 118 fights before they were considered professionals and were about 20 years old at their professional debut. It's safe to assume that they started their boxing careers around the age of 16. That means that those 118 fights were

---

18 "How Long Does It Take to Become a Decent Boxer?" *Quora*, http://quora.com/How-long-does-it-take-to-become-a-decent-boxer.

fought in the span of four years.[19] That's an average of 29.5 fights a year, or 2.45 fights a month. But they don't fear those rows because they have prepared for them.

In the same way a boxer prepares for the ring, so too must you prepare for your goals. If your goals are important to you, do what is necessary so that you can fight for them and give your all.

Goals are not reached in one day; they're reached daily. If you know in which direction to head and the path you ought to take, you must also know how to prepare. You can't claim you're aiming for your goal when you're simply sitting on the curb.

WHAT ARE YOU DOING TODAY TO GET YOU CLOSER TO YOUR DESTINY

Practice makes you better. *The level of your preparation determines the level of your elevation.* You can only go as high as your preparation allows. Preparation is the evidence of your belief that your dreams can be reached. Opportunity also awaits those who are willing to lay the groundwork for themselves. There may be people who have better resources, better educations or better methods to train and ready themselves, but don't let anyone have a greater willingness to know and a better disposition to grow. Preparation will show the day you need to glow.

---

19 Ivanov, Dimatar. "How Long does it Take to Become a Pro Boxer? Data from TOP boxers." *http://shortboxing.com/how-long-does-it-take-to-become-a-pro-boxer/*

Preparation is the key that opens the door to opportunity; it's the one who answers when opportunity calls. Greatness is more connected to preparation than to opportunity. That is why I truly believe in Gary Player's saying: "The more I practice, the luckier I get."

The reality of this quote is not the luck part, but rather the preparation part. I've come to realize that the more legwork I have done, the more opportunities arise. Before you go up the mountain, you have to take the necessary steps to ready yourself to climb it. The key questions are these: *How are you preparing? Is the preparation you're invested in the one that will lead you to your dream?*

Preparedness must be navigated with wisdom as its guide. Wisdom knows what to prepare for and, more importantly, how to prepare for it. The difference between success and failure is a matter of knowledge and understanding. Those who cease to train and better themselves are people who think they have finally arrived or those who don't know where they're going. People who dream of tomorrow prepare themselves to move forward.

You cannot embark on a journey without taking proper measures on the front end. In the journey of life, you can only walk in the direction of your preparation.

A WAR GENERAL MUST KNOW TO THINK AND FIGHT

In December 2019, my dad and I went on our annual father-son trip. This year, we went to China. Traveling is an adventure embedded in our walk. It expands our minds and our abilities to visualize. This trip, in particular, was an incredible adventure. From the city of Chengdu, we took a bullet train and found ourselves in the city of Xi'an.

One of the places we wanted to explore was the site of the Terracotta Warriors. The story told about these soldiers is incredible. They were discovered on February 2, 1974, near Xi'an by Zhao Kangmin, a farmer who became a curator for a museum. I had the opportunity to meet him and learn more about his incredible find. Desperate for water in the middle of a drought, some farmers dug a hole about three feet deep and unearthed these stunning historic treasures.

The Terracotta Warriors is a collection of more than 8,000 life-size sculptures depicting warriors and horses, buried near the first emperor of China of the Qin dynasty, Qin Shi Huang, in the year 210-209 BCE, to protect the emperor in his afterlife. It was a full phantom army with cavalry, horses and chariots, hidden underground and never seen by people. Today you can find these sculptures at the Terracotta Warriors Museum (Emperor Qin Shi Huang's Mauso-leum Site Museum). Since the year 1987, it has been considered by UNESCO as a World Heritage Site.

The terracotta army was buried in battle formation in three pits, approximately one mile east of the First Qin Emperor's tomb mound, which is also about 20.5 miles east of Xi'an. The three pits are between 13 and 26 feet deep. They have been excavated, and a hangar has been built in the ruins creating the Museum of the Terracotta Army.

Our excellent guide submerged us in China's history and its stories. We got to one of the pits where, aside from soldiers, chariots would deliver commands to the soldiers from the command quarters; the command quarters were where the army commanders would assemble to develop their battle strategies.

In the middle of her narrative, the guide mentioned that the generals had to possess two qualities: be great thinkers and skillful warriors. When she said that, my curiosity awoke and I asked, "Why did they have to be skillful warriors if what they needed was their ability to think?" I truly wanted to know because they could have been great thinkers with good ideas to employ in battle, even if they were not skillful warriors.

Her answer made me think. She said, "If you were a commander, you would be in the strategy room. The enemy would try to attack that place first in order to confuse their rival. That is why commanders had to not only be able to think, but also know how to fight."

Being a great strategist requires you to know how to think but also how to fight. That is why thinking is not a substitute for preparation, and preparation must always be accompanied by thinking.

Thinking and fighting are two characteristics a war general must possess, and in the fight for your dreams—for your goals—you must develop both as well.

PREPARATION KEEPS YOU CALM

Strength is the ability to stay calm, though the world around you may fall—to reinvent yourself though everything around you is looking to discourage you. Calm can only be achieved when the mind is calm, and the only way to accomplish that is through preparation, which dismisses fear and helps people think better.

Miyamoto Musashi,[20] a man who fought in 61 duels and didn't lose a single one, is considered the best samurai of all time. In his book, *The Book of Five Rings*, he talks about the importance of a calm mind for a warrior. He goes on to say that a warrior can only achieve a calm mind through practice.

In life, no matter our preparation, you may come across situations that are beyond your control. Maintaining a serene mind can help you conquer the unexpected. It's normal to have unforeseen encounters on the bridge to your destiny; that is why you need practice every day along the way.

When the unanticipated crosses your path, preparation must not be set aside. Those unexpected moments are what Musashi calls "critical passages." He writes:

> Here is what I call "getting over a critical passage." I will take the example of navigation at sea. In certain straits the currents are fast, and a distance of forty or fifty leagues constitutes a critical passage. Also, in traversing life, a person encounters numerous critical passages.

> In navigating at sea, it is necessary to know the dangerous places, the position of the ship, and the weather. Without having a pilot

20 Musashi, Miyamoto, translated by Bennett Alex. *The Complete Musashi: The Book of Five Rings and Other Works: the Definitive Translations of the Complete Writings of Miyamoto Musashi—Japan's Greatest Samurai*, 2018.

ship, it is necessary to know how to adapt to each situation. The wind might blow from the side or from behind or even change. You must have the determination to row for a distance of two or three leagues in order to reach port. That is the way you can get over a critical passage in a ship at sea.

This way of being also applies to traversing life. You must get over a critical passage with the idea that this event is unique. It is important during a combat of strategy, also, to get over critical passages. You get over them by precisely evaluating the strength of your opponent and your own capacity.

The principle of this is the same as for a good captain who is navigating a passage at sea. Once the critical place has been passed, the mind becomes calm. If you get past the critical point, your opponent will come out of it weakened, and you will begin to take the initiative. You have then practically already won. In group strategy and in individual strategy, it is essential to be determined to get over the critical passage. You should examine this well.

Musashi also adds that "spontaneity of the moment is necessary in battle." However, one can only be spontaneous when one is prepared. Crossing the bridge to tomorrow requires constant preparation in the present, for your future deserves you to fight for it with all of your today.

In *The Art of War*, Sun Tzu states the following: "Water shapes its course according to the nature of the ground over which it flows; the soldier works out his victory in relation to the foe whom he is facing.

Therefore, just as water retains no constant shape, so in warfare there are no constant conditions. He who can modify his tactics in relation to his opponent and thereby succeed in winning, may be called a heaven-born captain."

Situations can change instantly, but consistency helps us in any difficulty. Life is unexpected, but with the right preparation, you can win a battle to any destination. Practice gives us both the instinct to know what needs to be changed amid adversity and the flexibility to know which movements to employ to move toward the goal and win the war.

PURSUE YOUR GOAL PREPARED TO WIN

It doesn't matter what happened yesterday; today is the day when you must prepare yourself to fly away in the direction of your dreams. The past never determined a person's destiny; only the present can do that. The glory of victory is found in the daily routine. When you don't prepare for success, you're preparing yourself for failure. When you stop pursuing what you desire, what you don't desire enters your life.

You will never achieve a goal you do not pursue. It's like successfully reaching the end of a path you did not intend to walk. Both to reach and achieve you must maintain your stride.

Dreams are not only sought; they are fought for. The battle is not won the day you fight for it; it is won on the days you train for it. If you know which path you must take, it's a good time to prepare. Just as planning is ideas in action, preparation is acts in motion. Keep fighting, keep preparing; your future will thank you for having done so.

Just like many others, I have made mistakes in the past, and there are many things I wish I had done differently. However, what I regret the most is not having started my preparation sooner. The good news is that it's never too late to start over. Each day, each hour, each minute and each second is a new opportunity to make my life better. Do not wait for a distant tomorrow when opportunity awaits at your fingertips today.

What are you doing today for your tomorrow? What are you preparing yourself for? If you know what you want and how to obtain it, you need preparation to attain it. There may be people with greater talent in one area or another, but no one will fight as hard for your dreams as you will. What do you need to prepare for? When are you going to begin?

Just because I plan what I'm going to eat today doesn't mean my food prepares itself. Just because you plan how to attain your goals doesn't mean preparation should be dismissed. The difference between greatness and smallness is not found in your headset; it is found in your mindset. There is no limit to what you can achieve in the future when you start to prepare today.

REFLECTION QUESTIONS

1. According to the goal I want to achieve, do I know how I should prepare?

2. When am I going to start?

3. What am I doing today that brings me closer to the goal?

4. Can I be more intentional about my preparation?

    _____

    _____

    _____

    _____

5. What am I doing today for my tomorrow? Is that in which I am preparing myself today leading me to the tomorrow I imagine?

    _____

    _____

    _____

    _____

MAY TIME NOT BE THE ONLY ONE TO LEAVE ITS MARK;
IN YOU; MAY YOU ALSO LEAVE YOUR MARK IN TIME.

XAVIER CORNEJO

Time

"*The two most powerful warriors are patience and time.*"

—LEO TOLSTOY

To be a great strategist, you must also be a time master, for it is time that gets us closer to fulfilling our goals. What is more, it doesn't matter how old you are, the time has simply gone too fast.

I assure you that today, when you woke up, be it 19, 39 or 79, you are the age you are. The years you have accumulated are your own. Yet looking back on your yesterdays, many may seem like a distant memory. For some, it may even feel that your younger self was a different life altogether. Things we thought would never change have changed. Those we thought would always be by our side are no longer there and the wounds we thought we would never heal from are now scars that in some cases we don´t even remember.

Time continues to turn, and suddenly we find ourselves standing in the present, not even knowing how we got here. All the same, here we are. If we're not careful, however, we will wake up tomorrow, and all of our dreams, goals and desires will have been left in the world of possibility without ever becoming a reality.

I like to insist that your use of time is actually the use of your life, that your ability to enjoy your days is your ability to enjoy your life. A great strategist needs to possess the ability to know how much time winning the battle will take and have the wisdom to find the opportunities that exist at this precise moment in time to use time in the best possible way.

NEVER BE SO BUSY WITH ONE MOMENT IN TIME THAT YOU FORGET WHAT YOU WISH TO OBTAIN OVER TIME

Time is one of life's most valued riches; it's something you cannot buy, but you can indeed spend. It's interesting to think that we all have the same amount of time each day, but not the same amount of days to spend that time. Tomorrow is never guaranteed. Your time is finite. Given that reaching your goal and crossing the bridge will take time, be vigilant not to waste yours. Generally, the greater the goal, the more time it will take to get there. Each moment you allow to pass by is a moment you will never get back. That is why I mentioned before that the use of our time is the use of our lives. *Never be so busy in the moment that you forget what you want to reach over time.* We live under the paradigm that we do not have time, but there is always time for the things we truly care about.

If you have a painful toothache, you will try to go to the dentist as soon as possible. One way or the other, you will open up your schedule to go simply because you don't want to suffer. So, when we genuinely care about something, we have the capacity to make time for it. If you sincerely want to reach your goals, you need time to develop and employ your strategy.

Pursuing what you truly care about should never be left for another time, for it may get lost in the course of time. I really like Edwin Louis Cole's words: "Fame can come in a moment, but greatness comes with longevity." In other words, greatness requires time. If you're reading these lines, you still have time, and this could be your moment. When you plan your strategy, time must be an essential element.

I find it interesting that we expect things to grow 100 percent, but we only devote 10 percent of our time to it. How can we expect to reach 100 percent of our goals if we only give them 10 percent of our time? If you want to reach the mountaintop, you have to invest the time to climb.

Important aspects of time are how we manage it, how we divide it and how we use it. You cannot control it; you can only make use of it. Use your time wisely, and in time it will make you wise. Tomorrow will be the result of how you use your time today.

Don't worry about yesterday. Worry about what you will do today to reach the place that you long for in your tomorrow. The past has never defined a person; only one's daily decisions can do that. *A better future is built with what you do with your* time *today*.

KNOWING HOW MUCH TIME

There are two ways to employ time every strategist must consider. First, you must know how much time it will take to reach your desired end; if you don't, your expectations will be mistaken. Wrong expectations lead to lives consumed by frustration. In order not to give up because you didn't reach the end in time, you must consider time calculations from the start.

Marco is one of my best friends, a great doctor with a successful practice. The other day, while we talked, I asked him how many years it took him to study medicine. His answer astonished me; he said his studies in medicine took him 14 years. Fourteen years! That is a lot of time! How many times have I become frustrated with the amount of time my goals have taken me, and yet, none of them have taken me 14 years.

This gave me a fresh perspective for my life. I asked him how he studied for so long, to which he responded: "From the beginning, every medical student has a lot of anxiety and worry for the number of years they must study. On average, with subspecialties, a medical career can take from 10 to 18 years, and it's difficult to know exactly how long one's specific career will take. It brings fear because that is a lot of years that you depend on your parents, and it's hard to work and make money to support yourself. That makes a lot of people give up in the process.

"In my case, I knew from the start that I wanted to be a gynecologist, which helped me have clear goals, understanding that it'd be a long road, but someday I would reach my goal. It's much easier to handle the number of years when one goes into it with determination from the beginning to be a specialist, because you estimate how much time it will take you. In the last years of my area of specialty training, I focused on minimally invasive surgeries, and I had the opportunity to perform robotic surgery. When I graduated as a gynecologist, I became interested in cosmetic gynecology; it was something new and innovative at that time. I saw the opportunity of becoming a pioneer in that field in Ecuador."

I asked him if having the knowledge of the time it would take to complete his training from the get-go helped him have peace, to which he responded, "Of course, making calculations from the beginning helps keep you calm and eliminates anxiety. Planning was very good in my case."

If he was able to spend 14 years walking to cross the bridge to his goals, it doesn't surprise me that today he is a very successful doctor, an example for many of us who want to give up before we reach our promised land. He is a soldier who went to war for his dreams and came out victorious. Today he is decorated for standing firm in that battle.

Knowing how much time it will take gives me the peace I need to keep a steady pace. One of the worse things when it comes to pursuing our goals is not knowing how much time it will take to reach the place we aim for. Time will not always be exact, but an estimate can be a frame of reference, and knowing this from the start can help us not grow desperate.

INTERPRETING THE MOMENT

Secondly, knowing the time requirements helps us find opportunities bestowed by this very moment. Today is the best time to learn and undertake something new; there are so many opportunities no one knew before. *Knowing how to interpret the time is knowing how to maximize your life.*

I got a call from my good friend Marcelo. It was a pleasant surprise to get a call from him since we hadn't talked in a long time. I must highlight the fact that this call was in the middle of the COVID-19 quarantine. We talked for almost four hours about many different things, but one conversation was about his business and how he's facing these difficult times. He told me neither had been affected at all.

His company is called CMEsmartlife, a business with more than 30 years in the marketplace, which started as an operation of electrical infrastructure networks. He told me that over the years, the company has reinvented itself and expanded to include new lines of business. Today they do illumination design, audio, video and automation. He explained that as part of their culture, they have always chosen the best factories for their portfolios. He told me that when it comes to technology, one must always look for "the next thing." That allows them to look at trends over time rather than a single moment in time.

He proceeded to tell me that though they don't create anything, they constantly update their knowledge and services through the factories they work with. It is there where they find new opportunities for today and the future.

As of right now, they believe one of the industries that will be affected the most is the movie theater industry, so they're trying to help people create their own theaters at home. That is how they discovered Kaleidescape, a company that creates that experience through a screen and audio and through a server that houses all newly released movies available to the market, at the same time as the movie theaters receive them.

The Kaleidescape server doesn't need the Internet for people to be able to watch movies. They're stored directly in the server, with the highest picture quality and the best sound possible. It truly creates a theater experience at home. The purpose is for people to have a theater experience without having to leave their homes, so they can take better care of themselves during the global pandemic we're currently experiencing.

He doesn't only look at trends over time; time allows him to interpret the current moment. It wasn't long before things got more interesting. I asked him what the company's vision was. He replied: "The medium-term vision of our company is to be a leader in the *premium* market of illumination solutions and automation (audio, video, security, automation)."

Then he told me that their long-term vision is to have an international presence to provide logistics and support services for companies similar to them. I was surprised by the clarity of his answer about their medium- and long-term goals, so, naturally, I asked what time spans pertained to medium and long term for him. Once again, his answer was very clear: Medium term is three years, and long term is five years. He is a visionary who can interpret the moment, but he is also aware of the time required to reach his goals. I'm sure he will achieve them.

In the Bible, we find a very important reference to the sons of Issachar. They are only mentioned once, but what is said about them is so profound that I would like for that to be said about you and me. They were referred to as "*men* that had understanding of the times, to know what Israel ought to do."[21] A great strategist must constantly observe the times to know what things exist in the now that can help him achieve his goals. Today, there are more opportunities than yesterday, and I'm sure that tomorrow, there will be more opportunities than today. Being aware of each moment in the "now" can help you transition into what's to come.

Crossing the bridge takes time, and it's how you use your time that will determine how long it takes to arrive. At the beginning of your strategizing process, you must always plan and understand time. This will help you arrive at the moment when your goals have been achieved, your wars have been won, and your dreams have been fulfilled. Time will also present new opportunities that in your first steps were never contemplated.

FOOTPRINTS OVER TIME

Don't grow desperate to reach your goal; grow desperate to maintain the rhythm of your walk. Time passing does not necessarily mean one

---

21 1 Chronicles 12:32

is advancing. Sometimes, the best use of time is to pause, rest, breathe, think and then resume the walk.

When you don't give up along the path, you will leave footprints, and your achievements will inspire others not to give up—to persevere even when they wish to disappear. May your successes reverberate with the passing of time. May the path you travel shine for all those who follow the light. The echo you leave over time will lead others to find their chance.

Time is fleeting, but though a second can be over in an instant, it can help those who are consistent. Eventually, you will find that time has passed, and goals that used to only exist in your mind are finally part of your life. *May time not be the only one to leave its mark on you; may you also leave your mark on time.*

We need to learn to project ourselves over time rather than in a single moment in time. Those who focus on a single moment will be frustrated when the moment passes by, but those who project themselves over time will grow and cross the bridge to faraway lands never imagined but always desired.

A good strategist needs to have the ability to know how much time it will take to win the battle at hand. He needs to have the wisdom to know how to manage his days so that they lead him to the victory that leads to glory. Simply because the horizon is within sight doesn't mean you will reach it without a fight.

How much time are you investing in this moment, hoping you can reach your heart's longing?

THE BRIDGE

Goals require time to come to pass. Crossing the bridge to our goals will take hours, days, years, sweat and often even tears. However, when you get to tomorrow, the pain will lie behind you, and bliss will surround you.

Time can be a friend or an enemy. Which one it will be is not up to time, but up to you to decide. Make time your ally; when you reach the other side, you can say time flew, and you did too. Perhaps, your flight even spared you a walk because instead of crossing the bridge walking, you did so flying. If you don't use your time wisely, though, time can become your enemy, and instead of leading you to your desired end, it may lead you to your expired end.

With time as your enemy, you will never reach your destiny, but with time as your ally, you will obtain victory in every battle that comes your way.

REFLECTION QUESTIONS

1. How long will it take me to win the battle for my dreams?

    _____

    _____

    _____

    _____

    _____

2. Have I ever calculated how long it might take me to reach my goals?

    _____

    _____

    _____

    _____

    _____

3. Am I prioritizing my dreams?

    _____

    _____

    _____

    _____

4. How much time am I investing right now to achieve what I long for?

_____

_____

_____

_____

5. What are some tools available for me at this time that can help me conquer my dreams?

_____

_____

_____

_____

WHEN WE MASTER EXECUTION,
WE WILL MASTER VICTORY.

XAVIER CORNEJO

Execution

"Innovation is rewarded. Execution is worshipped."

—ERIC THOMAS

Execution is the art of carrying out the steps I planned as I attempt to reach the place I foresaw. I call it an art, not merely to use a fancy word, but to describe one of the most difficult phases in strategy. In August 2016, I had the opportunity to attend the Global Leadership Summit in Chicago, Illinois, in which I try to participate every year possible. It's a conference that allows me to grow, a place where I can nourish my mind and expand my knowledge.

One of the lectures that caught my attention the most was given by Chris McChesney, co-author of the bestseller *The Four Disciplines of Execution.*[22] One of the sentences that caught my undivided attention

---

[22] McChesney, Chris, et al. *The 4 Disciplines of Execution: Achieving Your Wildly Important Goals.* Free Press, an Imprint of Simon & Schuster Inc., 2016.

and I still remember to this day was the following: "There will always be more ideas than execution capacity."

No matter who you are or the size of your team or your company, there will always be more good ideas than there is execution capacity.

If you look back, you will realize that many of your ideas never materialized due to a lack of execution. That is precisely why executing our ideas or plans is an art. How many ideas or plans have you had that remained simply ideas and plans? Where did they go wrong? Was it the idea? Was it the planning? Or was it that you never executed them?

THE ENEMIES OF EXECUTION

TOO MANY OPPORTUNITIES

Far more dreams die because of lack of action than lack of planning. One of the most significant problems is that often, when we are in the middle of the execution of a plan, new ideas and new plans begin to emerge, and suddenly the end we'd hoped for becomes a rabbit trail to another place, and we never seem to reach the end. One *of the greatest enemies of success is not the lack of opportunity but rather having too many opportunities.* Each new opportunity robs execution of its strength.

While I was doing an Instagram live with my friend Joan, who kindly invited me to join him, the topic was "I finished my manuscript. Now what?" Many people interested in the publishing world joined the conversation, and one of the topics we had planned to cover was the difference between publishing with a traditional company and self-publishing. During the conversation, I explained that, from my experience, a manuscript is not always rejected because of its content or lack of quality; there are other reasons.

For example, at Whitaker House Español, we only publish 24 titles a year, two per month. With the team we currently have, we know that is what we can handle and give each book the time and attention it needs. We could publish many more, but we would be diminishing each book's opportunity to shine. Therefore, sometimes we have to reject manuscripts because we already have lined up all the books we need.

The question is: How did we decide to only publish 24 titles a year? The answer is: We tried doing more, and we always ended up having issues with execution. So, having too many opportunities doesn't always lead to success; sometimes, it's a path that slowly leads to failure.

LACK OF EFFECTIVENESS

My friend Melissa is one of the smartest people I know. Not only that, but she also has the capacity to notice details, which is quite admirable. One of her most remarkable qualities is her ability to make things happen. She used to be a general manager and buyer for a chain of souvenir shops that sold clothing and tourist articles. At the time, the chain consisted of nine stores.

Melissa led a group of a hundred people, and she told me that in her role as a buyer, she always planned where each thing she bought should be placed in the store. She even said that often, she would go to the store herself to verify that duties were performed correctly and that everything was where she had imagined they would be. Without the execution of her vision, the goals wouldn't be met.

Success hangs on placement, and generally, that's not a buyer's role. The buyer imagines where the products are placed, how they're displayed and how they should be sold. If the steps of execution that follow planning are not effective, purchases become an expense instead of profits.

DISTRACTIONS

There are far too many enemies of execution, especially in the world we live in today. It is a world full of distractions. In his book *Free to Focus*,[23] Michael Hyatt cites a study performed by a group of researchers at the University of California who found that "workers averaged twenty-five minutes to resume a task after an interruption like an email or phone." Hyatt goes on to say that if that worker is interrupted five times a day, as a result, he or she would have more than two hours lost.

In Scott Halford's *Activate Your Brain* book, which I mentioned earlier, he says that "one hour of well-focused time is equivalent to four hours of time rife with distractions." He goes on to say, "Once you have willpower and focus, it's time to learn exactly how to set your goals."

DELAYING

Everything around us competes for our attention, and often we *sacrifice the execution of what is important to resolve what is urgent.* That's not to say that we should ignore what's critical. On the contrary, I want to say that we should pay *greater* attention to what is important. There are several reasons why we leave things for later. Many psychological studies have been conducted to determine why we delay what we need to do.

---

23 Hyatt, Michael S. *Free to Focus: A Total Productivity System to Achieve More by Doing Less.* Baker Publishing Group, 2019.

In the book *The Productivity Project*,[24] Chris Bailey cites Timothy Pychyl, a psychology professor at the University of Carleton in Ottawa. He says that six attributes make delay more likely: boredom, frustration, difficulty, lack of structure, ambiguity and lack of personal significance. The more of these attributes the task has, the more likely we are to delay it.

LACK OF MOTIVATION

Another study[25] notes that we depend primarily on our self-control, which pulls from our motivation when we need to do something. Sometimes, there are demotivating factors such as anxiety and the fear of failure, or perhaps we see the end result as something so distant in the future that we disconnect from the rewards we will attain, and we lose our motivation to carry out the task.

But something we must understand is that tomorrow is not a faraway land, but rather a nearby destination. I think days reach us faster than we reach for the days. Often, I delay things when I think they will take too much time or will require me to think deeply in my own life. What works for me is to stay connected to the future I envision, knowing that each step's execution in my strategy gets me closer to my dreamed reality.

Don't lose your motivation! Try to focus your attention on what steps to take to secure tomorrow's success.

TOWARD THE ACTION IN EXECUTION

24 Bailey, Chris. *The Productivity Project: Proven Ways to Become More Awesome*. Piatkus, 2016.

25 *Solving Procrastination*, http://solvingprocrastination.com/why-people-procrastinate/.

SET DATES AND ANSWER WHO WHAT AND WHEN

Execution is important because it makes goals reachable and dreams achievable. When talking about implementation, it's vital to have an action date for each step of the plan. One of the most valuable teachings I've received from Sam Chand is the consideration of three words that must always accompany execution: "Who, what and when?" In Sam's terms, "Who's doing what by when."

When we work with our team to reach a goal, we must always know who's doing what and by when. Action is what makes the plan work. When we work toward a personal goal, it's also helpful to know what we're doing and when we will do it. Setting a date makes our dreams become goals, and they stop being mere desires.

It's not what I see; it's what I imagine that gives me a clear vision. However, to cross the bridge, I must also walk and not only imagine. Maybe you've been stuck in a moment. But when you keep walking, you will not be stuck in time. You'll see, though, as you start walking, that single moment in time will no longer keep you hostage. The present becomes past when a second has vaporized; the future can be certain when you add vision, planning and execution to the equation.

Clarity inspires us to see beyond to what no one else sees, and it compels us to feel what no one else feels. Planning helps us think what no one else thinks, but only execution can help us reach what no one else achieves.

If we are not willing and committed to walking, planning is not even worth a thought. Destiny awaits on the other side of the bridge; it's farther down the path. Think and plan; then, act and walk. *If you don't give up when faced with adversity, it will yield to opportunity, and that will turn possibility into reality.*

PRESSURE IS A FRIEND OF EXECUTION

Having a deadline for the execution of our plans is the best way to guarantee its fulfillment. Nowadays, people think that pressure works against us. We all live under pressure, and to some extent, the pressure is good for execution.

Edwin Louis Cole used to say about guitar strings that a lot of pressure can break a string, but a little bit of pressure tunes the string. In the same way, we need to have a little bit of pressure to set our plans into motion.

When it comes to our organization, it's best to surround ourselves with people who are good at execution. I tend to focus on the vision, on dreaming and on imagining. I have a more challenging time with the execution of many things. What works for me is having a team with a tremendous capacity for performance. In fact, often, I am the obstacle to their execution.

On my team, there are people with strengths and abilities I do not possess, and I can confidently say that in our organization, the things we achieve are largely due to my team. They propel me forward, applying the adequate amount of pressure to turn our execution into a beautiful song instead of an out-of-tune chord.

Today's pressure is tomorrow's precision, and I'm not talking about living a stressful life. I am referring to achieving the goal in mind. It's like a school or college assignment that is due in a month. Generally, unless it's a group assignment, we complete it a day or two before the due date.

The reason is that the due date applies the pressure that allows the execution of the plan. At least, that's how it was for me when I had to submit assignments in school, college and university. It's like doing on Sunday your homework that's due on Monday—even though you had the entire weekend to do it. Pressure is friends with execution.

It's a bit more complicated when it comes to personal goals because it's hard for us to set a deadline. We say we will lose weight, but we will start on Monday—and that Monday never arrives. We say we are going to pursue our dreams, but that pursuit never begins. It's difficult to put pressure on oneself. Somehow, it's easier to regret not having started than to pressure yourself and begin.

ACCOUNTABILITY

When we're talking about execution, my best recommendation is to look for a coach or a person who can hold you accountable. In my case, every Monday I have to send a report to the president of the company, which holds me accountable for my work. That weight on our shoulders can help us keep our feet on the ground and run toward the goals mapped out. You will be surprised to see how much you can achieve when you have someone who puts pressure on you.

It is said that a goal is only a dream until it has a deadline. The problem is that when we set the limits, we will always push them farther out because we don't have to report to anyone about the pursuit of our dreams. That will only take us to the end of our days, where we will find ourselves tired and filled with regret, lamenting we never crossed the bridge in the direction of our desired destination.

I have a friend whose name is Jim Davis. He told me the story of when he visited Sir Edmund Hillary, a great explorer from New Zealand and the first man to climb and conquer the summit of the world: Mount Everest. During his visit, Jim asked Sir Edmund what his greatest regret in life was, and he said the following: "One day, after one of the explorations to the North Pole, I saw a mountain I wanted to climb, but I was so tired that I said, 'I'll do it another day,' and unfortunately, I never did."

TAKING OWNERSHIP

By now, I'm sure you know how much I love my son Lucas. He is a light that illuminates my world, and he is the joy of my days; I'm certain that I learn more from him than he learns from me.

Like any good father, I think I notice his strengths more than his weaknesses; however, there is something he needs to learn and that is knowing how to take ownership of his failures. In the short seven years of his life, perhaps like every other kid, he doesn't own his shortcomings. It's always someone else's fault. In every game and activity, he always blames someone else for his loss. He has a hard time taking responsibility for it. I'm sure that if I'm not able to teach him this, at some point, life will.

Like Lucas, many of us go through life blaming others for our failures without understanding that our lives are our responsibility—executing the strategy to reach our goals is our responsibility. No one can do it for us; no one can enjoy it for us either. People will rejoice with us in our achievements, but achieving is up to us.

In the workplace, you can achieve things as a team. It's important to have a unified team that fights to reach the organization's goals and dreams. Often, it's those people who give us wings to fly and reach the sky. On a personal level, it's harder because you won't always have a team focused on your dreams; in those situations, the wind beneath your wings comes from within. At the end of time, what you achieved, or did not reach, will be your responsibility.

In your last breath, you won't be able to blame someone else for not having reached your dreams. Blaming others or blaming life will never be a good excuse for not building with your days everything you aspired to.

How many things we set aside in life because we're so worn down! How many regrets we carry within because we failed to execute our heart's deepest longings! I don't want to get to the end of my life only to face the regret of not having fulfilled everything I had ever dreamed. In your mind and in your heart, may there be enough pressure to push you forward in the direction of everything you have treasured in your imagination. Sometimes, we are our dream's worst enemy. When we do not execute, we sabotage what we truly desire.

REFLECTION QUESTIONS

1. How many ideas or plans have I had that have remained only ideas and plans? What went wrong—the ideas or the execution? Why didn't I carry out my plans?

2. Am I trying to execute more than one idea at a time? Could it be that too many ideas are robbing execution of its strength?

3. Is there something distracting my focus from executing my ideas? If the answer is yes, what is stealing my focus?

4. When am I going to execute my ideas? Have I set a date for the execution to begin?

_____

_____

_____

_____

5. to Whom am I accountable for my execution? To whom am I accountable for my life and where I am on the road to my dreams?

_____

_____

_____

_____

YOU CAN ONLY RISE FROM THE ASHES
WHEN YOU EVALUATE WHY YOU GOT BURNED.

XAVIER CORNEJO

8

Evaluation

"To win the battle, you must stop—breathe— but most importantly, you must evaluate."

—XAVIER CORNEJO

You can only rise from the ashes when you evaluate why you got burned. Similarly, I can only understand why I fell when I analyze what I tripped on. There is depth in the moment in which Adonis Creed confesses to Rocky, "I don't even know how I lost." It is in the nature of the comment. It's a moment of evaluation. It's this conversation that allows Creed to understand how he lost, but at the same time, it's at that very moment when he discovers how to win.

THE ONLY WAY TO PROGRESS IS TO ASSESS THE PROCESS

If we evaluate where and why we lost, we can also find the way back to our path. If I can understand what led to my defeat, I can also understand what can lead to my victory.

One of the most powerful moments in our lives is the moment when we ask ourselves these questions: *How did I get here? Am I where I want to be?* The pursuit of your goals must begin with an evaluation of your situation. Evaluation is the process through which we measure the success of our planning, our preparation and our execution. Evaluation allows us to know where we are with regard to where we want to go. *That which cannot be evaluated cannot be improved.* Evaluation helps us identify what is working well and what is going wrong. This is how we know how to make the necessary adjustments to move forward.

In order to adjust the sails on my boat, I need to know in which direction the wind blows. If I don't stop to evaluate in which direction the wind is blowing and in which direction the current is flowing, I will never be able to adjust the sails that lead to the unveiling of my destiny. The only way to improve is to evaluate; improvement must always be our aim.

I recently had the opportunity to have lunch with my friend, Ed Preston. During our conversation, we talked about his chain of restaurants. He told me he now has 25 restaurants—*Biscuits Café*—and more than 350 employees. Based on his experience, he said that three things make a restaurant successful: excellent service, good food and cleanliness. He then gave me a very interesting fact: Between 75 and 80 percent of his business are returning customers—people who had a great experience and kept coming back.

He didn't have to tell me, but the only way for him to know that percentage is because he and his staff evaluate their restaurants. If people hadn't assessed the business, they wouldn't know from where their income is generated. *Constant improvement comes from* perpetual *evaluation.* Life should be a continuous process of evaluation since evaluation allows us to adapt and adjust our planning, preparation and execution.

Where did I get off track? Where does my destiny lie? If we don't pause and take a closer look at our footprints, sooner or later we have to end the journey. An essential part of achievement is evaluating where I am with respect to my goals. It's when I come to know if my planning, preparation and execution fulfilled their role. *The only way to have progress is to evaluate the process.*

EVALUATING HELPS US IMPROVE

Many of us walk through life blindly simply because we've refused to allow evaluation to give us sight. I will not grow tired of saying that evaluation enables us to improve. Sometimes, the best way to improve is to stop, analyze and think about where your path lies. Don't live in fear of evaluation; it could save you from your situation. To appraise is to progress because now you know what to improve, what to change and what to adjust.

Evaluation is part of the bridge that takes us from possibility to reality. You will never be able to upgrade that which you are not willing to evaluate. *Evaluating the progress can help us improve the process.* Constant evaluation can lead to significant improvement. Lack of assessment can lead to the failure of your progression.

I know the word evaluation often produces fear because it reminds us of tests teachers used to give in school, college or university or evaluations at work that could cost us our job. But the true purpose of evaluation is to help you reach a new level in your life. If you have prepared, you won't fear the test.

EVALUATION TRANSFORMS US INTO MASTERS OF OUR PROGRESS AND APPRENTICES OF OUR PROCESS

It's time to be the masters of our dreams. If you don't evaluate yourself, who will do it for you? In the school called life, you play both roles: you are the master, but you are also the apprentice. *We will always be the masters of our progress and the apprentices of our process.*

We must learn to live in that duality and with that mentality. Take some time to think about where you are and what you need to adjust to cross the bridge. If you don't stop to consider your footprints, how will you know you are following the right path? Evaluating oneself is an intrinsic journey—a necessary journey—to adjust what is not functioning. Only you know where you are as it relates to your goals.

Let us be honest with ourselves because we will be the ones to enjoy the blissful sight of arriving at the place where our dreams are fulfilled. It's often easy to deceive ourselves on the daily path thinking that we are doing everything we ought, but it's only when we look back that we are able to see where on the path we got off track.

Interestingly, *life is lived toward the future, but it can only be understood toward the past.* It's in looking back that we come to understand what we are doing. Life passes by too fast for us not to stop and evaluate our path—not to yield lamentation, but to achieve performance optimization.

Evaluation

The battle of life must be evaluated if victory is going to be celebrated. Reaching the goal requires fighting, evaluating, adjusting, improving and persevering. The best soldiers appraise their abilities before the day of battle. Victory is dependent upon the evaluation that preceded the battle and continued throughout.Every combat strategist knows that the intention behind the first attack is to assess the enemy's abilities. It's in the second or third attack where, after measuring my enemy, I come to understand the strategy I must employ. Evaluation allows one to have information that could prove to be a vital tool in the fight.

How well you gather information can determine if your mission is a success or a failure; the wrong information is worse than no information at all. If your goals and your dreams are important to you, evaluation will be also. It's the only way to know how much you have progressed and the distance left to cross the bridge.

Take a moment to evaluate where you are today. Perhaps you realize you are not where you had hoped to be. However, as you measure yourself, you will see how much you have achieved. The beauty of life is not found only in the greatest moments that may come our way, but also in the small details of every day. If we do not evaluate our days, we may miss the beautiful moments that silently waited there.

Evaluation teaches us that a bad second is not a bad minute. A bad minute doesn't make a bad hour. A bad hour doesn't mean a bad day. A bad day is not a bad month. A bad month does not lead to a bad year, and a bad year does not mean you have lived a bad life. Despite everything you have faced in the past, walk onward, and fix your sight on what's to come.

No one can stop a person who walks with the conviction that life matters—that the future is secure—because, while there may be difficulties, they have the ability to keep moving even when everything is fighting against them. The ability to walk in spite of difficulty is called courage.

When you evaluate your life, you will realize that you are worth more than you thought you were worth and that you can achieve more than you thought you could achieve. You only need to carry into the future that which you desire to see there. The path to the future is a journey, and you need not carry a heavy burden. When the past ceases to be heavy, you can walk through life freely. Nevertheless, you have survived 100 percent of the battles you have faced, and here you are, ready to fight again to reach the end of the path that leads to your promised land.

Evaluation gives us essential information, not only about our input but also about our outcome. It's time to evaluate your footmark to know if you are walking toward your goal. I know we don't always like to evaluate, but it's the only way to elevate. Goals are not reached by mere desire; they are rewards to people who work hard and perspire.

REFLECTION QUESTIONS

1. How and when will I evaluate the progress of my execution? What am I going to evaluate?

2. When was the last time I evaluated the result of my strategy?

3. How did I get here? Am I where I want to be?

4. To whom should I be accountable for my evaluation?

    _____

    _____

    _____

    _____

5. What can I adjust to improve the steps toward my dreams?

    _____

    _____

    _____

    _____

WHAT MAKES YOU A
WINNER IS WALKING
DESPITE THE PAIN.

XAVIER CORNEJO

9

The Pain in the Path

"The one who knows about pain knows everything."

—DANTE ALIGHIERI

When we think about strategy, we must consider that pain is going to pay us a visit and that it will be part of our path. Simply because the past was painful does not mean the future cannot be blissful. Pain is a sign that you are still alive—you are still on the path. Only those who cease to live cease to suffer.

You cannot reach the bridge you expected without taking a single step. It's difficult to walk when you can imagine the end, and you must wait to get there. Everything worth reaching takes time. Every worthwhile achievement requires time. Every great story takes time to tell. Every step on the pathway gets you closer or farther from your destiny.

Life is not an event; it's a process. Goals are not reached in an instant; they are reached by being consistent. On our lane, there will be moments of pain. Pain is part of growth; pain is part of life. Giving up because it hurts is the worst mistake we can make, and when we give in, we cut off our wings. Walking, breathing and waiting are allies that accompany us on the pathway to our destiny.

The pathway to our goals is long, it takes time and it requires courage. There are moments of stagnancy that hurt, but the days keep trickling in, and life goes on. Stagnancy is not definitive unless you decide it is. Yes, it hurts, and yes, it's difficult, but it's worth it to keep going. *The pain of the path is nothing compared to the agony of giving up.*

The pain of failing will never be as great as the regret of not starting. Satisfaction is the result of overcoming pain. Just because you cannot see the end doesn't mean you cannot reach the end.

What makes you a winner is walking despite the pain. A soldier can feel fear, but he cannot let fear paralyze his feet because the war depends on him. The battle for your future rests on your steps. Fear can make you linger on a thought, but it should never cause you to stop. Your destiny is too important to stay halfway along the pathway.

Stay your course no matter what you have to confront. We cannot choose the enemy to fight, but we can choose how to fight. May your footsteps lead you to wisdom to welcome each new day.

Pain is part of life; it will find you on the path even when you pause. I personally prefer to be in motion; I have the feeling that I can break through my ceiling. *Every mountaintop takes time to reach and strength to climb to the peak.* I would rather attempt and bleed than stop and weep. Though tears cloud my view, they can never stop me from reaching the destiny I'm meant to embrace. In the same way that rain cleanses our world, our tears clean our soul, and only after the tears are gone do we discover how strong we really are.

The only reason you feel pain is because your lungs are still taking in air. I hope that when you look back at your life, regret may be nowhere in sight. I know that moving forward can be painful, but regret can consume your joyful elation.

I remember clearly the conversation I had with my Uber driver on November 16, 2019. I had just left the Mosaic conference in Los Angeles, California, and I was on my way back to the hotel. She mentioned how hard her life had gotten. For some reason, she'd had to adopt her sister's children and had recently broken up with her partner. Therefore, now she needed to pay all of the bills herself, and she was having a hard time.

Suddenly, when it was time for me to get out, I found myself saying these words to her: "Everything is going to be okay, and your days are going to get better. Pain also adds beauty to our story." Many times, when I go through a difficult situation, I have a hard time maintaining that perspective. I've come to realize, though, that the night also adds beauty to the scenery. It's not always daylight, but the darkness of the night cannot stop tomorrow's light.

THE LIFE YOU HOPE FOR IS ON THE OTHER SIDE OF WHAT YOU OVERCOME

Falling is only final if you don't get back up. As long as you can get to your feet, you can still walk. The light of hope will shine brighter on your boldness with each day that approaches. May your hope never cease to shine so the world can always see your light.

Pain is part of the journey, part of breathing and, above all, a critical part of growing. That's why we must learn to live with it. Those who overcome pain overcome the limitations that are hidden within. *It's better to gaze at the future with eyes of hope than linger on the* past *with yearning and remorse. The life you hope for is on the other side of what you overcome.*

Use the waiting to prepare yourself because the higher the summit, the steeper the climb. One time, I was with Sam Chand in the mountains of Ecuador, and he asked me if I could help him record a video for his leadership program titled "Tuesdays with Sam Chand." When I started recording, he began teaching. After the greeting, he explained to his audience where he was. He proceeded to tell them that it was harder to breathe at that altitude. Suddenly, he said the following words: "There is always less oxygen at the top."

He then talked more about the topic, how sometimes we think that when we get to the top, things will be easier, without realizing that when we get there, it's harder to breathe. When you get to the summit, there is less room to move, and the margin for error narrows because you could slip and fall at any moment. Additionally, the higher you are, the more painful the fall. The adventure of life resides in the details, whether good or bad. Each morning, sunny or cloudy, it's a new opportunity to dream again and to walk again. I'm not saying to pursue moments of pain, and I don't mean to minimize what makes your heart ache. What I want to say is that when you look back from the other side of the bridge, you will realize that the beauty of your story lies in what you have overcome. The stories, movies or novels that we find captivating are not the ones where everything came easily; they are the ones in which the characters overcome the darkest and irremediable moments that make their hearts ache deeply.

Your future deserves the wait. Your future is worth the pain because tomorrow will bring you gain. Life ends when you close your eyes and you can no longer imagine anything else. May the hope of a better tomorrow be your companion as you follow.

Tomorrow will come—not for everyone alike—but that's okay because each bridge leads everyone to a different life. No one crosses the same bridge.

Waiting can lead to desperation, but it's in the waiting that we acquire all that we need to cross the bridge. The path is long and will take time. Enjoy each step on the way, no matter how near or far destiny awaits. Perhaps, one day, when we celebrate the end, we may realize that the steps that led us there were just as important as the end itself.

The truth is, we are never alone. I'm convinced that *our Creator is always with us.* We may not always feel Him in the moment, but when we look back, we can see His hand on us and for us. That is when we realize that we have never been alone. You may be familiar with the famous poem, "Footprints in the Sand," which recounts a dream in which a person saw two sets of footprints—one set representing his own and the other footprints left by Jesus. The dreamer noticed that, at one point, the two sets of footprints became one set, and expressed frustration that the Lord had left him alone at a difficult time in his life. The Lord explained to the dreamer that, in fact, those where the times in which He had carried the dreamer in His arms.

When you feel you have lost your way on the path of life, and you are trapped inside the labyrinth, look up. The stars can also be your guiding lights. No matter how tangible the dark becomes, there will always be light above: the sun, the moon or the stars, and behind them, you will find that God is leading you on.

In my life, there have been many moments of pain—moments I thought I had reached the end. However, when I look back, I realize that what I once thought was the end was simply God leading me to a new beginning.

REFLECTION QUESTIONS

1. Am I aware that pain is an integral part of reaching my goals?

2. Have I ever thought about giving up because of the pain I have encountered on my path? How has pain changed my perspective?

3. Have I reduced the size of my dreams because of the pain?

4. Am I willing to walk despite the pain?

_____

_____

_____

_____

5. What strategies can I develop to overcome the pain, knowing that the pain of not trying is far greater than the pain of continuing to walk?

_____

_____

_____

_____

THIS IS THE MOMENT TO DRAW
YOUR SWORDS AND FIGHT
TO SOAR TO THE SKIES
AND REACH FOR THE STARS.

XAVIER CORNEJO

10

Growth

"*We must war against the temptation to settle for less.*"

—ERWIN RAPHAEL MCMANUS

The more you grow, the more battles you overcome. More than reaching goals in life, have goals that take a lifetime. Those sentiments sound alike, but they are not the same. Growth must be a lifetime goal for all who seek to conquer their dreams. As time passes, we grow older, but we don't necessarily grow wiser.

Growing old happens with the passage of time, but growth happens when we maximize every moment in life. Time ticks for us all the same, but we are not all the same as time slips away.

Growth is a decision—a decision we must make each day. *Growth is the result of consistency.* You cannot grow in a day, but you must learn each day. *You can't grow on the outside until you have grown on the inside.*

To grow is to broaden your horizon. You will see farther down the path and find more bridges to cross and more views to admire. When you grow, your entire world grows, your team grows and everything you do endures. Growth is the remedy for stagnancy. A life devoted to development is a life that increases and soars. Growth is a choice that the heart must forge. *How much you grow will always be your choice.*

I think we can all agree that extending ourselves can lead to flourishing, and even more than that, it can lead us to new heights where we can soar and explore new horizons beyond. That is how we will climb new mountains, find new bridges to walk across and set new goals to go beyond.

If we understand that growing is important to obtaining higher achievements, why do we not always pursue internal growth?

HUMAN BEINGS HAVE AN INFINITE CAPACITY TO GROW

A couple of weeks ago, Lucas was playing in the street with other kids from the neighborhood. While we watched the kids play hide and seek, I struck up a conversation with one of the kids' dads. Suddenly, I found myself lost in an interesting conversation about the brain. It turned out this man is a university professor, and he had signed a contract with a well-known worldwide publisher in his field. The manuscript he needed to turn in exceeded 600 pages.

While he was interested in the fact that I work in the publishing field and wanted me to give me advice on the contractual part, I was interested in the topic he was writing about. His book is about brain imaging—images through which one can see the brain and its functions. We started talking about the different types of intelligence, and he told me how much of a role genetics play.

He said that, according to which part of the brain a person uses, one can lean more toward mathematics or law because, generally, we only know about the logical and the creative intelligences. The brain is so powerful that we can extend our way of thinking at any moment, and we can convert our intelligence from one to another or express them both. People who are essentially logical can be creative, and people who are creative can develop a logical intelligence. It takes effort, time, and strategy, but it's possible.

As we talked about Lucas, he also told me that the best age for a child to learn another language is until the age of 14. He went on to explain that until that age, the dendrite branches, which connect neurons, establish their patterns. After that age, it's very difficult (though not impossible) for them to detach and change the thought patterns. I asked if at any time it is too late for the brain to learn new things, to which he replied: "It's never too late, it may be more difficult, but it's never too late." Therefore, no matter your age, you can always increase your ability to grow.

Carol Dweck confirms this. She is a psychologist and researcher from Stanford University who describes herself as follows: "My work bridges developmental psychology, social psychology and personality psychology, and examines the self-conceptions (or mindsets) people use to structure the self and guide their behavior."[26]

---

26 Dweck, Carol. "Carol Dweck." *TED*, http:// ted.com/speakers/carol_dweck.

In her book *Mindset*,[27] she developed the concept that there are two types of mentalities—growth mentality and fixed mentality. After much research, she discovered that most successful people are the people who have a growth mentality. She describes it in the following manner:

> In a fixed mindset, students believe their basic abilities, their intelligence, their talents, are just fixed traits. They have a certain amount and that's that, and then their goal becomes to look smart all the time and never look dumb. In a growth mindset, students understand that their talents and abilities can be developed through effort, good teaching and persistence. They don't necessarily think everyone's the same or anyone can be Einstein, but they believe everyone can get smarter if they work at it.[28]

People who have a growth mentality don't care about looking bad or failing because they know that is part of growth. They keep developing, and they keep fighting. They never stop trying no matter how many times they may fail.

This is the type of mentality every one of us needs to practice. I think a person's talents and abilities are limited, but a person's ability to grow and expand is limitless. When you navigate new seas, you will need new skills as you will discover new lands to conquer and new people to encounter. At the end, steady growth will lead you to what you're longing for. The sky will never be the limit for those who aim to reach the stars.

---

27 Dweck, Carol S. *Mindset*. Robinson, an Imprint of Constable & Robinson Ltd, 2017.

28 "Fixed Mindset vs Growth Mindset: How Your Beliefs Change Your Behavior." *James Clear*, Feb. 4, 2020, http://jamesclear.com/fixed-mindset-vs-growth-mindset.

THREE THINGS PROMOTE GROWTH

You can always grow, and it is never too late to learn and try something new. Three things have helped me grow: curiosity, capacity to extrapolate and conscience insight.

Curiosity opens the way for opportunity. A child breathes curiosity. That's why we should not be surprised by the speed of a child's growth. Children always want to know "why?" and they don't mean to annoy us. They ask it with sincerity, and that genuine desire to learn expands the frontiers of their knowledge.

One of the biggest enemies of growth is that, with the passing of time, we stop asking "why?" We come to accept everything. We are responsible for constantly limiting curiosity when we say things like, "Don't be so curious," or "Stop snooping around and get to work." *When we limit curiosity, we limit opportunity.* Extinguishing our curiosity is like cutting off the wings of our freedom to explore, seek and advance.

I learned from my friend and coach Héctor Teme[29] a truth that I have not forgotten since he shared it with me: "The answer closes; the question opens." I also learned from him that an answer is simply the result of ceasing to ask. That said, the actual problem is that our curiosity isn't usually purposed for our growth, but rather our knowledge—not to know about things that could help us, but rather to know someone else's secrets.

We must direct our curiosity to something that can help us grow. Curiosity paves the way for discovery. Everything man creates is the

---

29 Founder of METODOCC, author of *Lo que los exitosos piensan* (2020) *y Punto de partida* (2019), Whitaker House.

result of curiosity, of seeking the "why" of something and then taking what we discover and giving it shape and form so that we can share it with others.

CURIOSITY MAKES A WAY FOR GROWTH

In 2012, my friend Carolina went to study at the Basque Culinary Center in San Sebastián, Spain.[30] She was already an incredible chef. During that time, she met Iñaki, her boyfriend, who is also her business partner. Five years after having finished her master's degree, they opened their own restaurant called Ikaro[31] in the city of Logroño.

The concept of their restaurant is a fusion of Ecuadorian cuisine with the cuisine from the Basque country (where Iñaki is from) and La Rioja, where the restaurant is located. When I asked Carolina how they decided on that style of cuisine, she said they wanted to put their roots on a plate and for their personalities to be reflected.

They specialize in gourmet cuisine where they highlight traditional techniques they like and respect.

What makes two people from two completely different places try a mix of what they know individually and what they don't know? Curiosity! The only way to awaken a world of possibilities is through curiosity. In order to decide on a dish to be included in their menu, they

---

30 Basque Culinary Center (http://bculinary.com) is a pioneering academic institution worldwide. It houses a Faculty of Gastronomic Sciences attached to Mondrago University and a Center for Research and Innovation.

31 "Restaurante Ikaro: Restaurante Gastronómico En Logroño La Rioja." *Ikaro*, http://restauranteikaro.com/.

try their mixes of flavors several times. As Carolina says, "We try five times—sometimes more—in order to approve a dish as final."

Their curiosity to explore a style of cuisine that didn't exist led them to win the prestigious Michelin star in 2018, which is given to restaurants for their excellence in three different categories. They got a star precisely for their creation of a completely different concept. The best part is that they didn't even expect it, especially so soon after having opened the restaurant. They only had been open for a year and a half since their inauguration, and it's very rare for a Michelin star to be given to a restaurant that new, unless it belongs to a famous chef.

I asked Carolina where they saw themselves in the future due to the challenge of surpassing a Michelin star. Her answer surprised me because I could feel the greatness of her dreams and passion in her pursuit. She said the following: "As a result of the star, other projects have emerged. We've opened a new restaurant in the city of Logroño, and we are thinking about opening something in Ecuador, which would be a dream come true. We are restless (curious) people, and we like to keep growing professionally, but without a doubt we will not neglect Ikaro, which has brought us to where we are today."

I've yet to taste the greatness of their food, but as I write this story, I feel the greatness of their hearts. They are people whose curiosity opened the doors to places they could never have imagined. This is what curiosity can do for you. I promise that as soon as I can, I will go and try their food. I have a feeling that what they make is more than food—it's art; it's life. If you're ever in the area, you need to go to their restaurant. I'm sure that their food will inspire you to dream as well.

Give yourself the opportunity for curiosity to lead your steps; it's on that path that growth, learning and enduring will come about. Curiosity is like a heartbeat that leads you to seek a cause that will bring growth. Many times, it's curiosity that opens a window for your purpose to set in. I strongly believe that curiosity is your destiny calling your heart; you need to answer its call so that you can keep moving along.

Seek to always cultivate a close friendship with curiosity, for it will lead you on a path of venturing out into unexpected adventures and delights. Let the adventure lead the way; the more you venture out into the world, its places, flavors and lessons, the more your curiosity will awaken, and when it rises, your life will rise as well.

THE CAPACITY TO EXTRAPOLATE EXPANDS KNOWLEDGE

I enjoy extrapolating, which is basically learning principles from a different industry and applying them to yours. Miyamoto Musashi used to say, "From one thing, know ten thousand things," and in his book, he repeats the following: "To know ten thousand things, know one well."

Many patterns repeat themselves in all professions. I've mentioned it before: It's what you learn differently that makes you different. Seek to learn always and in every moment. We never get to a place where we can say we have learned all, and if you think you may have gotten to a place where you know everything there is to know about your profession, start asking how things work in other professions. Then you will learn things that no one else is learning, and you will be able to do things no one else is doing.

Each day, as you walk, as you watch and ask, you can multiply your capacity. We can learn a lot from complex theories, but we can also learn from steps we take each day, from morning to evening. Always ask yourself: How can I use what I learned here? Is there anything from this profession or process that I can use in my career?

A few weeks ago, I had the opportunity to visit Xochimilco, a borough in Mexico City. In 1987, Xochimilco was declared by UNESCO as a Cultural Heritage of Humanity. It was a wonderful adventure that I shared with a group of endearing friends. We explored the canals on a colorful and fun boat.

They had told me that rowing in that place is very difficult, and at one point during our ride, I approached the young man who was rowing, and asked him how one must row in that place. He showed me how the paddle must go into the water from a certain angle and how it should be pushed when it hits the bottom of the canal. Then he showed me how to turn and how to move forward.

Suddenly, in the middle of our conversation, he said the following: "Once you learn the theory, then you can develop your own techniques." Without knowing it, that young man was giving me a lesson that can be applied in any other area of life: *Before developing your own techniques, you must learn the theory.*

Much of my growth has been the result of learning processes from other industries and applying them to mine, and many times they have been remarkable discoveries. *Extrapolation is connecting the points between what you observe in one place and what you can do in your place.*

An example of this is the principle of balance that operates in the architectural interior. A perfect design entails the concepts of harmony, space, scale, proportion, transition, emphasis and repetition. All of that is framed in the balance of materials, textures, colors and saturation. The fundamental principle to reaching perfection or success in a design is balance. In business management, the same principle of balance applies.

Finance experts and businesspeople perform an analysis of benefits where the following elements need to create a certain balance in order to produce success: risk analysis, cost of products or services, prices, salaries and others. There needs to be a balance between investments, profits and all factors involved.

CONSCIENCE INSIGHT INCREASES WISDOM

The third thing that causes us to grow is conscience insight. We all experience the world differently because we all have different experiences in the world. Learning and having insight into our experiences is an intentional process. One cannot only learn from experience; *it's necessary to analyze the experience to extract the lesson.* My recommendation is to have a diary of one's experiences and lessons learned where each time you learn something, you write it down. Afterward, you can study it and reach new heights. Insight is a great teacher that can show you how to conquer new battles, how to traverse the open blue skies, and how to cross the bridge to the other side, where your dreams can be found.

In their book, *Mind Gym*,[32] Gary Mack and David Casstevens present the idea of learning as one of the prerequisites for having a successful life. What they say goes hand in hand with learning from experience:

> Young people are often brimming with natural talent, such as a hardy constitution or an athletic physique. Yet, as we age, these natural powers begin to fade. With most successful people, this faltering body is replaced by a stronger mind. Drawing from all other experiences, their mistakes and successes, older people are perfectly positioned to learn the tips to staying successful.

Although lifetime experiences increase with time, lifetime wisdom doesn't necessarily increase with time. No matter how much experience you have, whether it's a little or a lot, reflect on your life, distill the gold from your days, learn from your mistakes and grow. Only then will victory be yours. There's a popular saying that says, "If only the young knew and the old could." You don't need to be old to learn from the experiences along the road; you can grow at any age and stage.

When I was in school, my teacher taught me that the cycle of life is to be born, grow, reproduce, and die. Without growth, you can't reproduce. In what part of the cycle of life are you? I'll let you answer that question.

BE A CONSTANT APPRENTICE

Who you become depends on where you invest. Your achievements and goals will never be more important than you are. It is of no use to reach your goals and cross the bridge to the other side if you haven't

---

32 Mack, Gary, and David Casstevens. *Mind Gym an Athlete's Guide to Inner Excellence*. McGraw-Hill, 2007.

grown within. The most important thing about a person is not his appurtenance; it's his permanence. *What is truly yours is that which you cannot lose.*

Reaching our goals is important; it helps us have a full life. What defines you, though, is not what you do; it's who you are. You can renounce what you do, but you can't renounce who you are. All of your achievements can fade away, but who you are will always remain.

Change is the only constant in life. Today you have, tomorrow you may not. The world spins around, but who you are will remain, despite seasons and change. If you are going to set goals for your life, my greatest advice is to be a constant apprentice—not a casual apprentice.

The future is forged by those who are constantly learning because today they know something they didn't know yesterday. Beyond that, they know things no one else does. *Knowing and growing always help doing.*

Constant learning is the shortest path to your destiny. My friend Dr. Dale Bronner taught me the following principle: "They don't pay you for the value of the hour; they pay for the value of what you add to the hour." To add value to the hour, you must learn and grow.

Learning helps you begin, which allows you to take wing. The problem many people have is that they want to do things backward: They prefer to run, then to begin and finally to learn. When people do things in that order, the learning cost will be higher. Learning always enlarges the landscape. Those who think they don't have the time to invest in learning miss out on the benefits people reap from greater understanding.

Growth

Your ability to see the future shouldn't be based on your capacity to remember the past, but rather on your capacity to embrace the present. This is because when you grow, your capacity and your ability will also increase. *Steady growth can help you have a strong life*—a life that challenges the limits of possibility and turns them into reality. Growing, learning and understanding are the elements needed to become all you are dreaming of. One of the most extraordinary qualities of growth is that it ends in stagnation only if you halt your determination.

Growth is imperative in life, so much so that even Paul, the apostle who wrote two-thirds of the New Testament, challenged us with his words to grow to the stature of the perfect man, who was Jesus. Paul's personal goal was to keep moving forward until attaining the whole measure of the fullness of Christ.

For me, growth is just as crucial as attainment. *If you devote yourself to growth, there is no bridge you cannot cross; there is nothing you can't achieve or destiny you cannot reach.* Growth gets us closer to the moment—the place everyone wants to reach—but few actually achieve. In that place, there is more beauty than you can ever imagine. It's a place where horizons grow wider, dreams turn into realities and bridges are crossed. *Paradise is on the other side of commitment.*

Your greatness is only limited by your decision to grow. If you are not increasing, you're decreasing. In a world that is constantly moving forward, you cannot remain the same. To face the greater bridges that tomorrow will bring for me to cross, I will grow.

GROWTH GIVES YOU THE WEAPONS TO CONQUER

One of the most important qualities of growth is that it diffuses fear. Growth scares away fear; the more you grow, the less fear you own. It's like when you study for a test, get ready for a presentation, rehearse for an audition, or run through your *song*. You're not fearful of the presentation. You may feel nervous, but never fearful. I always feel nervous before any talk I give or any manuscript I submit. I think nerves show that I have the desire to grow, and they also show the value and significance of what I want to do.

The great samurai Miyamoto Musashi, whom I have mentioned before, wrote the following[33]:

> I describe my school in terms of two swords, since all warriors, from vassal to the ordinary soldier, must wear two swords firmly at their sides. Formerly, these two swords used to be called *tachi* and *katana*; today they are called *katana* and *wakizashi*. It goes without saying that all warriors wear these two swords in their belts. Whether they know how to use them or not, in our country carrying the two swords is the way of the warrior. It is in order to make the advantage of carrying the two swords understood that I describe my school in terms of the two swords. The lance and the *naginata* are weapons to be used outside, on the field of battle.

---

33 Musashi, Miyamoto, translated by Bennett Alex. *The Complete Musashi: The Book of Five Rings and Other Works: the Definitive Translations of the Complete Writings of Miyamoto Musashi—Japan's Greatest Samurai*, 2018.

In my school a beginner learns the way by taking the large swords and the small sword in his hands at the same time. This is essential. If you are going to die in battle, it is desirable to utilize all the weapons you are carrying. It is deplorable to die with weapons left in their scabbards without having been capable of using them.

The battle for your goals, your dreams, your longings and your desires will require all of you. Growth gives you the weapons you need to conquer and win the battle for everything that burns your heart with desire; it gives you the ability your reason requires. This is the moment to draw your swords and fight to soar to the skies and reach for the stars.

If you are willing to take up the fight for your dreams, fight with all the weapons laid out in front of you. If we are going to die somewhere on our walk, may it be after we have utilized every weapon we acquired on the path. Let us fight for what we want with everything we have. At the end of the day, a warrior's honor is not in winning or losing; it is in giving his all to the fight he chooses to take up. To win the battle of life, your mind must expand and your abilities should multiply.

Growth is the empowerment of knowledge. The more you grow, the more bridges you will come to cross, and there will be no limitations to what you can pull off. Those who love you and whom you love deserve for you to fight with all your might, to use all the weapons you can gather and the strength you can muster because the battle of life deserves your all. Those who devote themselves to growth can go further and beyond.

THE BRIDGE

In 1968, John Stephen Akhwari[34] went to the Olympics held in Mexico. While he competed in the marathon that wound through Mexico City, around the 19-kilometer (11-mile) mark of the race, he fell. He hurt his knee and dislocated his hip, and his shoulder hit the pavement with grave force. However, he got up and continued running. He finished in last place. Only a few thousand people remained in the stadium, and the sun had already set.

A group of reporters that had been sent for the awards ceremony found out that there was a runner missing and that he was about to cross the finish line. When he finally crossed the finish line, a small group of people cheered him on. When he was interviewed, they asked him why he kept running. His answer was, "My country didn't send me 5,000 miles away to start the race; they sent me 5,000 miles away to finish the race."

I'm convinced that you were created by God and sent by God to this world not just to start the race; you were sent to finish the race. You have something that this world needs. There is a light inside of you that can illuminate the world and change the soul. *Don't give up when you hit the ground; don't give up when the pain is profound.* You may have been wounded, but you have not been destroyed. *You can only surrender when you have reached the other side of the bridge.*

The only way we can cross the bridge that leads to fulfilled dreams is when we have grown and become people who fight with everything

---

34 IOC. "Marathon Man Akhwari Demonstrates Superhuman Spirit—Olympic News." *International Olympic Committee*, IOC, 8 Nov. 2020, www.olympic.org/news/marathon-man-akhwari-demonstrates-superhuman-spirit.

within—for our desires and for all those whom we love and who love us in return.

To grow is to transcend. To learn is to expand one's horizons. Significant dreams are achieved with constant growth. There is no limit to what you can become and overcome if you just devote yourself to grow.

THERE IS NO BARRIER YOU
CANNOT SURPASS, BRIDGE YOU
CANNOT CROSS, GOAL YOU CANNOT
REACH, BATTLE YOU CANNOT WIN
IF YOU JUST DARE TO TRY

REFLECTION QUESTIONS

1. What habits should I establish to never stop growing?

   _____

   _____

2. Do I accept the responsibility to continue growing once I have crossed the bridge to my dreams?

   _____

   _____

3. Am I curious enough to keep growing?

   _____

   _____

4. What lessons have I learned lately, and how can they help me in my walk?

   _____

   _____

5. Am I willing to give my life to chase my dreams?

   _____

   _____

Quick Strategy Guide

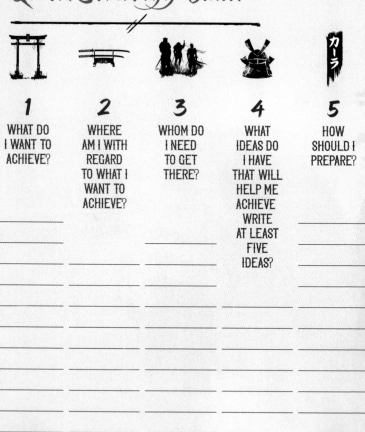

1	2	3	4	5
WHAT DO I WANT TO ACHIEVE?	WHERE AM I WITH REGARD TO WHAT I WANT TO ACHIEVE?	WHOM DO I NEED TO GET THERE?	WHAT IDEAS DO I HAVE THAT WILL HELP ME ACHIEVE WRITE AT LEAST FIVE IDEAS?	HOW SHOULD I PREPARE?

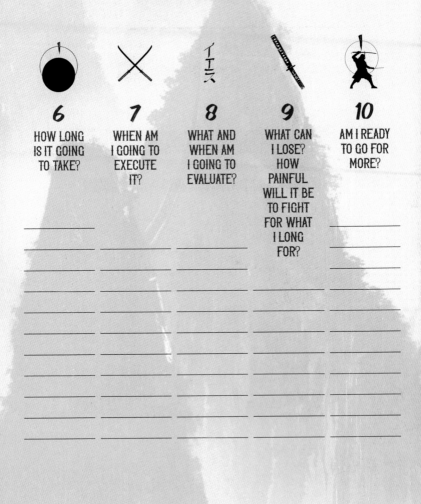

6

HOW LONG IS IT GOING TO TAKE?

7

WHEN AM I GOING TO EXECUTE IT?

8

WHAT AND WHEN AM I GOING TO EVALUATE?

9

WHAT CAN I LOSE? HOW PAINFUL WILL IT BE TO FIGHT FOR WHAT I LONG FOR?

10

AM I READY TO GO FOR MORE?

About the Author

Born in Cuenca, Ecuador, Dr. Xavier Cornejo is the award-winning author of *La historia dentro de ti*, a book praised as best first book and best inspirational book. His introspective vision has made him an icon in editorial wisdom and an influencer and solicited speaker in the publishing industry.

As the Director of Whitaker House Spanish Division, he has been responsible for the publication of more than 300 titles, including the works of Erwin McManus, Samuel R. Chand, Dale Bronner, Edwin Louis Cole, Michael Hyatt, John and Lisa Bevere, Steven Furtick, Donald Miller, Caroline Leaf, Jon Acuff, Jentezen Franklin and Tiago Brunet, among others.

With a doctorate in jurisprudence from the University of Azuay in Ecuador, he holds two graduate degrees from El Tecnológico de Monterrey. He is a senior coach at METODOCC. He was the executive director of the Sam Chand Leadership Institute and also presided over Zoegraf, an editorial firm in Ecuador, where he worked with authors such as Brian Houston and Edwin Louis Cole.

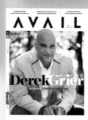

AVAIL
PODCAST

THE AVAIL LEADERSHIP PODCAST
HOSTED BY VIRGIL SIERRA